And They Ran

By

Jani Perry

Paperback ISBN: 978-1-959820-43-7

Hardcover ISBN: 978-1-959820-44-4

E-book ISBN: 978-1-959820-42-0

In accordance as registered with the Library of Congress in the United States Congress Office.

 Published by Author Ghost Writer. Buffalo Groove, Illinois.

Printed on acid-free paper.

Author Ghost Writer.
2023

AUTHOR
GHOST WRITER

Authorghostwriter.com

A Natural Heroine

This book is dedicated to my Grandmother.

Isabella Lee Harris

There is only a mystery of what a mother endures while pursuing the safety of her children. Madea derived from the name "mother dear" also known as (Gal) tells those among the descendants about love, rearing, and the impositions of intimidations that the Harris Family tolerates as their lives were entrusted by a society of disdain regarding the rights of humanity. This name does not personify the "Tyler Perry's" fictional character "Madea"; but this name is indicative of the relationship in most ethnic households meaning strength and support, honor and love. Madea taught her children to waste nothing but to offer kindness to their neighbors as one day that spirit of love would find itself back to them. As I listened to various narratives of my family's heritage, it became a legacy to me, a refreshing story, but a heartbreaking experience of one so dear to me, my grandmother Isabella Lee Harris who paved the way for all of her children to honor patience, kindness, and give a deaf ear to anger, and discord.

Table of Contents

Chapter # 1

The Struggle

Dark skies and gloomy days were the norm for her, with no timepiece or alarm clock, Madea knew exactly when to end her night's rest. She had the instinct that her parents passed from generation to generation that if she drank plenty of water at bedtime, she would make several trips to the outhouse during the night. Having the exact time at her disposal was not possible, but she practiced as to figure the approximate time by observing the moon's position, which enabled her to wake up on time.

There was no electricity, running water, or inside toilet. Madea kept a huge pot with a lid covering near the corner of their two-room shack. Her bedside table held the kerosene lamp as kerosene was an enormous commodity at this time. During the night, the family relieved themselves by using the huge pot as a convenience of not having to make trips to the outhouse.

Madea called the pot a slop jar; she takes the slope jar outside, dumps and cleans it before she awakens the children from their night's rest. She cleans the slop jar thoroughly with potash soap and well water and fills the bottom edge of the pot with remaining water and lavender fragrance for the next use.

As Madea returns to the house, she collects fresh water and gives herself a quick sponge bath as the water heats from the wood-burning stove. Grandpa draws the water from the well, bundles the logs, and secures the chickens prior to the family retiring to bed as he prepares for special emergencies.

1

Normally there was a pot of oatmeal on the fire prepared for breakfast; instead, Madea rushed the mere toddler and the breast-sucking youngster by washing their faces as they lay and sponged their little bottoms, hastily dressed the children and herself. She packed the food to feed the children at the work site so she would not lose any time for fear of bad weather.

June was a time of abundant harvest because the crops were plentiful, and there was a time to settle crops with the property owner, as there were many tenants gathering the food. With two children at her side, Madea managed her workload in the field, as sharecropping was the families' source of support.

Necessities were a luxury for the family, such as dental needs and other personal items. Madea fed and put the oldest asleep and carefully laid the child, wrapped in a patchwork quilt inside of a huge open-faced burlap sack that had a considerable amount of padding. The child would lie as if riding atop a cradle onto the sack that she skillfully designed.

Although Madea was petite and of very small stature, she had years of fieldwork and therefore was in excellent shape. The burlap sack had double long twists on each side that purposely fit around Madea's waist in order to drag the child as she worked. The second child, crying uncontrollably, was ready to receive her breakfast as Madea removed her scarf, unbuttoned her blouse, and freed her breast to feed the hungry infant.

When the child finished nursing, her little head fell back in a sleep pattern. Madea helps the child to release a huge burp. The child lay cuddling in a warm blanket atop Madea's waist as in a shoulder sling while she performs her daily activities. Madea harvests the land as needed until night approaches and collects whatever food is available in preparing the supper. Madea never complains; instead, she makes this type of operation a way of life as there is no question of a babysitter in their lives.

As the children grew, the breast-sucking infant stopped sucking from her mother's breast milk. The load became less burdensome for Madea when the youngsters fit safely together in the burlap sack, allowing her to relinquish the shoulder sling blanket from resting atop her waist. "Now I make more steps, pull more peas." Each day, Madea works on the land and comes home to take care of her husband. She prepares his meal and comforts him intimately.

Grandpa, without any intent, plays a small role in the life of his family and contributes little because of multiple partners and outside children who add to Harris's bloodline. This kind of extramarital affair was very prevalent among Negro families because the men would set out to hunt and fish when they were off for long periods away from their natural families. Madea never forgot to give thanks and prayers for her family and neighbors. "

I work this land because my lord gives me the strength to feed my babies." Having no more than a third-grade education with little reading or writing, she somehow made things doable and kept going. Faithfully, she attends a church when fellowshipping with others as they took an interest in providing help to her in overcoming illiteracy as she began to write her name and study her bible.

Madea always walks miles and miles to and from the plantation when making her rounds as the children nestled together in an antique carriage that she found near the plantation.

This carriage salvages from the wreckage that housed needful things such as clothing, consisting of bloomers, handkerchiefs, and ragged linen. She was very skillful in repairing or redoing usable items as she washed and made abandoned items look new after providing special alterations.

Madea always says, "I knew that this was a blessing from heaven." She has always shown docility and never complained, but she is always far-sighted and discerning. She observed and explored ways to provide for her family those needy things that were otherwise unaffordable.

The children's carriage was of extreme benefit. Madea made her rounds throughout the plantation, finding time to make homemade toys constructed of patchwork stuffed with cotton and buttons used as eyes, sewn on the mouth, and ears. The precious toys were as if Christmas had come early in the eyes of the little ones. The children always watched Madea as she cooked, cleaned, or darned their father's socks as if being in a training session.

Madea took pride in herself and the appearance of her children. She would separate Sunday clothes from the everyday apparel and say. "We're going to get out of our church clothes right now, so we don't get them soiled because we will be wearing them again."

Madea was a beautiful, brown-skinned Negro woman with long wavy corn rolls. When in the sunshine, there was a reddish appearance gleaming from her hairline. She never straightens or uses any relaxers in her hair.

In the evening, she and the girls would start a fire in the wood-burning stove, go out, and draw the water for supper and baths. After supper, Madea and the girls would prepare the bath water and climb into the large tin tub that accommodated the three. They bathe with oxygen soap, sometimes referred to as potash soap. Madea uses potash soap for bathing, cleaning the house, washing the clothes, and doing the dishes.

She and Grandpa had no way of birth control. After the children lay down to rest for the evening, Madea and Grandpa had a moment of intimacy. Madea tries to control her childbearing as the family is poor and does not have adequate means of childbirth. Grandpa and Madea gave restitutions to the midwives for their help; she never took for granted the kindness at a tender time during the birthing of her children, and she felt an obligation to give the gift of thanks and endearment.

Madea would remind her husband of how devastating it was to feed the existing family, but the lovemaking was overwhelmingly hard to avoid as she felt the irresistible desire for sex being a tinder young woman. "I love you, but I pray to the lord for us to have no more children." As she blew out the lamp, there was suddenly brightness from the moon with just enough light to remove her housecoat, exposing her naked body.

Her husband was very slim and tall with reddish brown skin, a descendant of American Indian and Negro also had soft, unkinked hair. He began to caress her very soft and tender brown skin without any future expectations. When they began to advance each other, he released his undergarment as the uncontrollable and serene passion filled the moment with heart-pumping pleasure.

The pulsations are hard to control to avoid awaking the little ones when there is only one room with the two bunks that separate them. Sometimes, when the climax occurs, it causes the furniture to squeak, and the two occasionally forget there are children. Madea never allows the girls to see her and their father without coverage during intimacy."

I contact you because we need one another. We got to find some privacy from the children".

Madea continues to cuddle with her husband. The lovemaking was never a hindrance to not getting up as planned. She beckoned for her housecoat as she passed the undergarments toward her husband, realizing the next few hours meant another workday. Madea always awakens on time with the same routine as the children and herself, especially if a rainy day is possible.

Madea and the girls would hurry out of the house for the day's work. As the children grew, their diets changed, and they began eating food like Gal and their father. Madea packed hog jowl and biscuits for the girls' breakfast with cane syrup and milk as there was no need for sucking from the breast or preparing oatmeal as left over supper was sufficient. Madea taught her girls to work hard and always put something back for a rainy day, even if it was a jar of mayhaw jelly or a slab of cured hog jowl.

When the owner divided the crops, Madea would spend hours canning her profit. She would put the canned goods up for a future need. Grandpa raised hogs and often picked a fatted pig for slaughter. This was also a contribution to the family's food source. On Saturdays, after the slaughter, Madea would invite her family and close neighbors for the scraps.

There was none thrown away, every inch of the meat was utilized. They cooked the fat of the pig in a black cooking pot that was made of cast iron. They cooked the hog skin into a very tasty snack called hog rinds or skins. The fat is also cooked to make oxygon soap. This was a time of Family Reunion and, therefore, began the family's yearly get-together. There were times when Madea was unable to work the field when she was the only baby sitter the family had when the girls became ill of a fever or stomachache.

Madea always thought a dose of castor oil and a piece of peppermint candy was a cure for all ailments. "I find a way to bring healing round this here house. Being around the house was a convenience as she would stop and nurse those who were ill. "Doses of castor oil with a chunk of pepper-mints-sweet make us better." Madea would collect her cast irons, as she would use them to do the laundry.

Madea gathered her basket, the girls, and her will to make things happen. She went out and brought in housework. Madea received fifty cents for a full basket of linen and garments. She heated water from the well after making several trips to perform her chores. The huge black cast iron pots were her washer with the assistance of grandpa. They placed the pots on top of a pile of wood, ready to fill with the well water.

They used oxygon or potash soap in the boiling process. With a huge fireplace match and safe handling, the wood heated the water, and the water pots began to heat. Madea carefully placed the clothes in the boiling water with a long bamboo pole.

As the clothes boiled, Madea would carefully jog and poke the clothes until the garments appeared clean. As the clothes washed, Madea used the tin tubs to prepare fresh rinsing water. Again, Madea would use the long bamboo stick to pluck out all the hot clothing. As the water-cooled the clothes, she would slosh and hand ring the excess water from the garments. The garments hang on several lines with clothespins in order to finish the drying process.

Madea made sure that she washed early so the clothes would be taken inside to be starched and ironed. She made her own starch by using a homemade recipe to starch the clothes. Madea used Argo starch and water to make the stiffening for searching. Each piece of clothing was carefully sprinkled and balled up so the starch would penetrate thoroughly. Madea often stopped before completing the work and prepared supper for her family.

After serving her family and putting the girls to bed, Madea went back to her chores. She collected the cast handheld irons and then thoroughly washed them. She heated the irons on the wood-burning stove until they were extremely hot. Madea made an area on the table where she used her linen to help with padding for pressing the clothing. Madea would iron all night until the work was complete.

The next day all the pieces were folded and ready to return with a fresh scent of lavender throughout the house. Madea: prepared for the next day, a pot of oatmeal simmering on the stove for the girls' breakfast, fresh squeezed orange juice, and a pot of coffee with biscuits, mayhaw jelly, and fried hog jowl for her and Grandpa. The family gathers around the table for breakfast this time, as there were no hunting trips or fieldwork.

Madea and Grandpa began to exchange ideas on how they would continue to provide for their family and feed the hogs. Grandpa had a strong will in his voice, but he often stuttered as the words came out very slowly. "Gal, them hogs a...ra...a going to be sold." Madea disagreed with Grandpa, as she knew the pigs were Grandpa's means of providing meat for his family.

"I' know us going to make ends meet without any hasty selling, I will oblige you when there was no meat in the yard. There was a long winter, but I honor your choice, and I shall be submissive to your decisions." Grandpa, firm in his decision and head of his household, made his point without any procrastination. "I a...ra ...been talking to a White feller about selling just two hogs and da...ra... that's a...settled."

Madea silently and obediently compromises with patience. She learned a powerful lesson in listening, loving, and letting go. She gave in and respected her husband's decisions as Grandpa, like Madea, had little education, but he was a good business dealer. "I take two...twenty dollars for my hogs." Madea smiled and said. "Wells to do," knowing that this was a done deal.

The family continued with breakfast as Madea poured more coffee into Grandpa's giant tin cup for his morning sips. The girls continued to eat their oatmeal and drank their orange juice. They were happy and anxious to get out and play after eating. The children, now toddlers, needed the help of their parents as the two- and three-year-old toddlers were too small to exit the tall steps without assistance.

After the house chores, Madea and Grandpa escorted the youngsters out to play. The children loved feeding the chickens and playing with their handmade dollies. Grandpa enjoyed this time with his family as hunting and fishing took a lot of time away from family life, and therefore, minimal time was spent with the girls.

As the day progressed, the family began picking abundant pecans throughout the plantation. Because of the supply of nuts, Grandpa and Madea were able to sell their profit to help with needful things. The girls began to get restless and needed a nap. Madea whispered in a gentle tone. "I suspect we need to put the babies to rest." Grandpa immediately dragged the nuts to the edge of the steps and tied the burlap sack.

He took one of the girls while Madea had the other, and the family went up the steps to the house. Grandpa, with Madea, had good premonitions of a boy child. He thought continuing Harris's name as a male baby would give him access to the family when there were masculine activities that only he could perform, having the upper strength of natural ability and of man persuasion.

Even though neither Madea nor Grandpa worked in the field today, spending that quality time with the children was full of accomplishment and novelty. As the girls napped, their parents had time for spiritual meditation. Madea knew that without her time in fellowshipping with others, she would not enjoy the intimacy of meditation. "We know whence' we praise Him blessings going to follow."

"I learned to read the words in the bible with my church families so we share amongst one another. "Grandpa was just a little more advanced in literacy than Madea, so she strengthened her inclination with his help and her will to ponder continuously. Madea observed the acceptance in her husband's whole atmosphere as the meditation finished. He was more forward to repentance.

"I love you, Louise Harris, and the children. I pray we are one family. "Madea knew Grandpa was not always faithful in his marital status, but her devotion and love for her babies gave hope as Grandpa's consensual advances with other partners and a possible outside family during his hunting trips were now non-existent. He makes his way back home to Madea and the girls. Holding back tears, Grandpa admits his wrongdoing.

"Gal, a... ra, I'll be true to my...woman, I will a...stop cheating." Madea and Grandpa began to hold each other passionately as they kissed and made eye contact. Together the two went quietly out to gather water for supper and baths. With the excitement of desiring attention, the children cried as Madea prepared the food.

Grandpa bathed the girls, and after the children's bath, he gently dressed them and placed them to the table.

Madea hastily sat at the table and put the serving utensils into the large pot that contained the stew. She made yeast rolls as if it was Sunday after church. The Family sat down and gave thanks for their meal. The next day, Grandpa sat out in attending his business deal with the White fellow. Grandpa sold the hogs and the money as promised. The White fellow paid Grandpa two twenty dollars for his prize.

Being a hog farmer, Grandpa was able to provide for his family. There was no hog slaughter around the plantation during off-seasons. No facilities were suitable to house or keep the meat from becoming contaminated. Madea continued to take in laundry, as the extra money would help when the food was bare and the hog supplies were low.

The price of materials for making her and the girl's clothes was outrageously out of the family's budget, but after consuming the flour, Madea would take the huge bags of and make her clothes. The flour bags came with an assortment of colorful floral appliqués. While removing the appliqués, Madea would gently and without raveling the delicate design places the precious emblem in a sewing case.

The girls have grown to be very active and playful. This was a time to assign chores for the little ones to keep up with them. "I done took us outside. It's time we feed the chickens and sweep the yards." Children given their special assignment were excited and ready to seize the moment. Madea's days had been a little slow; she thought there was a virus in the air.

She began to sleep longer and experienced some light-headedness. At breakfast, she confesses to her husband about the possibility of being with a child. "I ask the lord to stop my childbearing, but I guess this is his will." Grandpa smiled and began to embrace the gift of child he had made with her. With extreme delight, Grandpa felt just as responsible for expanding the family as his wife.

"Gal, a...ra just to let you know, I a...ra will be helping with them chores as I done with the other babies". Madea, always thinking of ways to feed her family, she kept going to the field with the assistance of Grandpa. Being pregnant with a third child, she continued to work. The drayman knew the Harris family was in need of eatable goods. He blessed them with food and stored the contents beneath the house.

Potatoes and other perishable items would appear beneath the floor. Madea would take the food and prepare their supper and canned all she could, as the food would be there when there is no work for the family. "I knew the Lord done blessed us." Madea was an excellent cook; everything she prepared was a delicious feast. "We got a little cane sugar, some chicken egg, flavor, and some flour."

With her loving spirit, Madea baked a delicious treat for the drayman. Madea wanted to give something, as this was an appreciation of the kindness shown to her family. Grandpa would borrow the neighbor's mule and buggy and load the cart with scraps of old soured grains as the family set out to feed the hogs. He knew that this was not the time of year to slaughter, but he, just as if Madea, remembered the kindness shown to the family when there was no work or hunting available.

The girls enjoyed the ride on the buggy as they sang and clapped their hands with Madea. Madea taught the children how to sing uplifting inspirational songs. After months of being with child, Madea gathered the necessary items needed for the midwives to perform their work for the delivery of her baby as she had this experience before. She washed and bleached huge towel-size scraps, as they were useful items.

Madea often crocheted as she had means of being in possession of supplies. "I make these foot shoes' to put on the child." Madea had a beautiful cedar chest that was a gift to her. She remembers her mother instilled great qualities into her as she folded all of her best things and kept them in a safe place for future reference. Madea saved all baby clothing and linen from previous deliveries in preparation for the oncoming family.

With enthusiasm and excitement, Grandpa polishes the cradle as it was used for the previous babies. Madea and Grandpa had no type of finance, but they stored food as a means of payment to offer when it was time to deliver their children. It was almost impossible for Grandpa to go on any fishing or hunting trips as Madea was deep into her month of delivery. Friends could not assist the midwife during the birthing because they lived demographically too far in terms of preparation and waiting.

The girls were so young and helpless in this type of situation, as they did not understand what to do. Grandpa and Madea made plans for the midwife to be in place. Grandpa, without any future desire for hunting or fishing, initiated the idea of helping when there was fieldwork, as Madea kept the children and contributed to what she was able to do in her condition.

Three weeks before the delivery of the child, the family imposed once again for the use of their neighbor's mule and buggy. Madea, Grandpa, and the children set out to fetch the midwife. With the experience of previous labors, Madea knew what to do even if the pain grew severe. "When this here child comes, he will get good treatment. I'm going to do what I can to bring' him here".

"With all the strength I got, I ain't letting any pain stop me". Madea has always been very resourceful. In natural birthing, she would assist the midwives by cleverly accommodating her help, knowing when to take breaths and push during delivery. There was no type of drugs to help in relieving the pain after the birthing. Madea made her own pain reliever, and she put it next to her bedside.

She prepared a brew that she occasionally used to relieve illnesses for her family. The concoction consists of aged blackberry wine and peppermint candy. Madea would only take this dose after the delivery. The wine would cause her to sleep as she maintained herself in having the strength to suck. It was a long and dreary day back at the plantation as the midwife and the Harris with the propensity to bring forth a healthy child there; Madea began to contract as her water broke.

The midwife measured the belly as they approached the shack; she knew the baby's timeless arrival could be detrimental during the phase of the birthing, but Madea was determined to fight like a soldier. The midwife knew that this might cause complications for mother and child.

Grandpa carried Madea up to the long steps and into the shack without a moment's interruption. The family did not expect an early arrival; with the excitement of traveling, Madea entered labor, and the child began to enter early.

Chapter # 2

Welcoming Johnny

Grandpa went out to the buggy and unharnessed the toddlers; they were fast asleep, unaware of all the excitement. Before Grandpa entered the shack, there were cries of a new baby. He was finally here. The child screams with extreme vocals after Madea, with the help of the midwife, finalizes the birthing while they wash the newborn as she extracts the afterbirth.

The child cried with exceedingly strong lungs, as Madea was weak with hardly any strength and barely catching her breath, "Please let me hold my child." she was tired from the long ride and the birthing and, therefore, began to lose consciousness. Grandpa took the baby, kissed and hugged the child as he adulated excessively, "I a... ra help makes a fine boy". He begins to name the child without conversing with Madea.

John Henry Harris, a name his father gave him, received the child and placed the newborn infant in the cradle as Madea woke from her restful quietude. There was a strain in her voice as she experienced afterbirth pain. "he hollered so much, it's times he got a-suck-in." The midwife checked Madea and the child. She was very impressed with how well the birthing had gone as the baby came early.

Madea softly spoke as she turned toward the baby, giving gratitude to the midwife; "thanks be to you, us really thanks you "Madea looked at Grandpa with sincere amazement and began to make conversation, "Us needs to name the child." Grandpa's response was so absorbed that Madea immediately knew that the baby had his name while she was at rest. "What have you named your son?"

Grandpa was so eager and proud; this moment meant the world to him. "Ara, he is to be called John Henry Harris." Madea, with all the pressure behind her, accepts the new name. "I like this name; I'm going to call him Johnny. "Madea begins to render hospitality to the midwife. It was suppertime, and everybody was hungry and tired from the trip. Grandpa took the pot of soup that was already prepared and heated the contents to a steamy, bubbly, delicious meal fit for royalty.

Grandpa prepared biscuits and placed them into the wood-burning stove long enough to warm the soft, melted, buttered bread. He collected the water from the outside well to freshen up and prepare the tea. After supper, the children had baths and were dressed for bed as Grandpa made provisions in lodging for the midwife when there was only a two-room shack.

"I need lots of quilts." Grandpa gathered the quilts and placed them next to the toddler's bed, and the midwife slept through the morning comfortably. After delegating and giving Grandpa special instructions, Madea receives the baby and holds the little one in a sucking position with the help of her husband as the child sucked until sleep was upon him.

Grandpa took the infant with an authoritative grip, burped and swaddled him, and laid the child face up in the cradle. "I thank you for giving me a beautiful boy." He kissed Madea and blew out the lamp. Early the next day, the child, hungry and wanting attention, cries out in selfish and needful rage. Everyone awakened, including the toddlers. The midwife took the infant, removed the soiled clothing, and gave him to his mother.

Grandpa prepared breakfast, brewed a pot of coffee, made biscuits, and simmered a pot of oatmeal for the toddlers. Madea planned to give goods that she and Grandpa had put away to the midwife for her diligence in helping with the delivery. Madea accepted no help in getting from the bed. She went unswervingly to the slop jar behind the quilted makeshift door, relieved herself, washed up, and sat with the others for coffee and biscuits.

It was time to get back on the road to take the midwife back to her home. "I suspect we are...being moving alone, don't be... being anything good about a...ra this we...weather." Madea, with her tailor abilities, stitched aprons and bonnets for the midwife, all fragranced, starched, and folded; there was an array of canned goods, homemade jellies, pecans, and beautiful hand-designed handkerchiefs.

"I was saving for this; didn't know how we were going to come by paying." Grandpa temporarily housed meat with chunks of ice; he gave meat, consisting of jowl and ribs, while the goods was being packed and placed in the buggy. The midwife thanked Madea and gave her blessings for the new addition to the Harris family. As she turned towards the outside door, she remembered writing the infant's name, sex, and nationality in a small bible.

Without recourse, she gave the bible to Madea with a blue ribbon inserted into a specific page. With the help of Grandpa, she climbed onto the buggy. Grandpa went around to the opposite side and climbed into the driver's seat, and away they went. Madea watched through the window of the two-room shack as the mule galloped unceremoniously and disappeared down the long dirt path. Madea was eager to get into a routine of being able to run her household without the awkwardness of pregnancy.

She had a lot of catching up to do, even with the nursing infant added to the workload. She wanted to continue her job as a laundry girl and house cleaner, taking in clothes and having the advantage of being around as a homemaker when everyone needed her. It was the middle of the day; Madea bathed the infant, sucked him, and dressed him from the garments out of the cedar chest.

The toddlers were very inquisitive and wanted to know where the baby came from. "Gal! Who is a baby doll?" "His name is Johnny. He ain't a baby doll." He's your 'little baby brother." "Where did he come from?" Madea answers very firmly and with no hesitation. "Well, he comes from Papa and me." Madea continued to clean the shack, wash the slop jar, and tend to the needs of the baby.

The toddlers wanted to play out in the yard with the chickens after the midday meal. While gathering the children to venture outside, Madea had to place the cradle on the ground and bring one child after the other down the long steps from the shack. There, the infant and the toddlers were out in the heart of the day, enjoying the sunny atmosphere. It was the middle of March as the pecans were ending their season.

The children fed the chickens and picked what was left of the pecans. Madea, still weak from birthing the baby, she knew the shack would be safer as the day lingered on and the toddlers all fidgety for a nap. "Us going be getting up the steps." Just as they came out, Madea escorted the sleepy youngsters back into the shack. After the children were safely in the shack, Madea laid each of the children at rest, washed up, and began to start supper.

Grandpa left everything at Medea's fingertips. The water was ready for cooking, bathing, and cleaning. As Madea cooked the meal, the aroma filled the air. The food was prepared early because the little one needed a lot of attention, and Madea had to utilize as much time as she had available. After the short nap, the toddlers awakened and were ready to assist Madea with the baby.

It was getting late. Madea looked out into the distance, and finally, Grandpa, with the neighbor, traveled back to the shack to retrieve the mule and buggy. Grandpa got out of the buggy, bid the neighbor farewell, and started up the steps. He entered the shack and observed how well the space was organized. The baby, the toddlers, and Madea all waiting for his return.

With hugs and kisses, Grandpa embraced his family as Madea set the table Grandpa while washed up. She placed the toddlers at the table, and they all gave thanks. It had only been twenty-four hours since the child's birth, and Madea was enthusiastic about comforting her husband and taking on extended jobs. With full obstetrical care, the midwife gave exceptional instructions, as Madea had to be in full compliance throughout the ensuing period.

Grandpa loved Madea and was very patient as her body continued to recover after birth. "I'ze be a ra taking to the field." Grandpa would work from sunup to sundown, making sure the family had the supplies needed for the new addition. He continued to raise and sell the hogs as his business grew and was able to make serious deals as he needed the mule and buggy to make extended trips. He knew his neighbor was in the process of selling the entire outfit because his of son's leaving for the military.

It would take all the hogs and more to make the full payment for the transportation. He needed seventy-five dollars to pay his neighbor. He only had three hogs after making a previous deal with the white fellow. Madea felt Grandpa's compelling desire to buy the mule and buggy and wanted to help. "We need the hogs for meat, but If us sell a female and a male us going to make a fine profit."

Grandpa was astounded as he listened to Madea! Grandpa realizes right then that Madea had the making of a great deal. The white man heard about the hog selling, he offered a decent deal with Grandpa as the female pig was pregnant. Grandpa received fifty dollars for his prize after letting only one hog go.

When the deal was final, the two hogs, both males, were left, leaving meat for the family. "I know the neighbor going to take this here because it's lots of money," Madea had spoken with confidence. Grandpa consulted the neighbor, and surely, he accepted the fifty dollars for the mule and buggy.

Grandpa and the Neighbor shook hands, satisfied and delighted. He drove the mule and buggy home; he could not wait to get back to the shack. The children had their baths and were all fast asleep, even little Johnny. Grandpa was so inspired to have accomplished two tasks in such a short time that he told Madea of his great day and how amazing her idea helped him in his business dealings.

Madea begins to remove supper from the wood-burning stove that she kept warm for Grandpa. "I kept some supper. I'm very pleased that you take to my word for your fine dealings. "Grandpa kissed Madea and hastily began to remove his coat. He started for the door, heading out to fetch water for his bath.

Grandpa finished his meal as the water heated on the wood-burning stove. Madea spoke with that unusual sentiment in her voice. "I will gather your bath and make it nice and bubbling for you." Grandpa knew that this was no ordinary loving-kind-ness situation; he saw into her eyes how much she needed him, that it was time to share that fervent and intense passion as two people desired.

Johnny was now five months old, and Medea's womb was in good health. There was no risk of infections; she followed all of the midwife's instructions. "I done obeyed every word the midwife spoke about." She began fondling his chest with light strokes, as his masculine physique was intense. Grandpa was just as passionate as well. While losing his belt buckle, he stuttered but in a very masculine and romantic nature. "Gal, I ...Need you, I'm a...ra ...going to be very careful."

Grandpa stepped into the huge tin tub and took Madea by the hand as she dropped her bed gown. They washed each other, and there they made love. The next day, Madea was back into her routine. It was early morning, and Madea loved getting a good start on her day as the breakfast was being prepared with little Johnny screaming for attention.

She stopped, picked the child up, washed, and gently clothes him. She sat in an old rocker that faced the window with the infant in her arms; she removed her breast, and with clean linen, she covered herself while nursing her baby. The girls were still asleep, even Grandpa, through all the commotion. Grandpa finally awakened, quietly got out of bed, robbed himself, and started toward the window where Madea was nursing the baby.

He nobly lifts her long, soft corn roles as she wears her hair and kisses her neck. Madea held her head to one side, welcomed the kisses, and continued to nurse the child. She burped the child as soon as he was done nursing, laid him in the cradle, and reminded Grandpa of the relaxing and exhilarating moment they shared last night.

"There is nothing like what we had last night; I love your strong arms holding my midsection. Grandpa gave her the kind of tenderness she desired, as she did for him. "I a ra want you to have everything your heart desires, because you're my life's treasure." Madea was still very young as they married when she was in her early teens, and Grandpa, in his mid-twenties, was merely responsible enough to take on an incoming family.

Madea did not see what the future would bring; as much as they loved each other and their children, adding more to the family would devastate their relationship tremendously. The girls got up to relieve themselves and had a sponge bath with the assistance of their father while Madea set the table for their early meal.

When breakfast was over, she warmly dressed the children because she had to collect the dirty laundry from her potential clients. This was a hunting season as Grandpa and his friends would team up and take to the life of game catching. They would stay as long as two weeks at a time as game hunting was part of the finance for their families and food source. Madea would spend some very lonely days alone when Grandpa was away.

She was not able to work in the field, but her job was near the shack, tending the children and doing household chores. The children were much bigger and more aggressive, and they helped with simple chores. They watched the baby while Madea prepared the ride in the buggy pulled by the mule. Madea gathered the children; everybody was off to collect the day's work.

She continued washing and ironing for the duration of the two weeks Grandpa was away. She washes all day and iron all night, a hard worker, is lonely, and needs to be held by her man. Madea fed the children each meal routinely and suckled the baby. Upon Grandpa's arrival, the girls unlaced his boots and scratched his head at the excitement of him being home from his hunting trip.

Madea cooked and watched the girls bond with their father; she was just as happy as the children were. Grandpa stood up, walked towards Madea, and kissed her passionately as if to thank her for all her diligence in caring for the children during his absence. "I Ara misses you and the children; I just want to a…ra…hold you." Little Johnny was very frisky; he had begun crawling when his father was away.

He would crawl up to his father's pants and brace himself while he pulled up. Grandpa reaches for Johnny, hugs him, and kisses him. "My little…man, a…ra you are going to be a pig slaughtering soon." The girls babysat while Madea worked in the yard washing laundry. They picked pecans, and the two children pulled the heavy burlap bag to the bottom steps of the shack, seeing that Grandpa brought surprises for his family back from his trip.

Each girl had their very own doll and a new pair of boots; even little Johnny had his first pair of boots and a teething ring. "A...ra I know money a...ra must be saved, but a...ra when I go hunting, I make a decent deal for a...ra my game. He presented *Madea* with a precious piece that fits around her neck and a new long white laced gown with blue and lavender appliqués.

Grandpa brought a supply of meat and grain for the hogs and chickens, plus candy for the children. Madea was pessimistic about the future, as she put back something in case there may be a sudden drought in food shortage, "I love you, my darling husband us must put some savings away." Grandpa wanted to give his family things; he wanted to repay the times he missed spending with his only son while hunting, that quality moment with his family by spoiling them with fine gifts.

Madea had decided that their family was complete when little Johnny came along. There was one thing the midwife did not give in the instructions, and that was protection from conception. Madea loved Grandpa and wanted to make him very happy, but she feared that there might be another child soon. She became depressed and absorbed in her chores while Grandpa worked the fields getting ready for the harvest.

Little Johnny was still nursing as Madea gave him soft puree food from the table to supplement his growth. It was late December; Johnny had taken his first step. Madea thought, "They tell me if a child walks earlier than normal, then they make room for another baby. "Johnny was very aggressive and fast; he was nine months old, walking and playing with his sisters.

Because of the workload Madea created for herself, she was unable to submit to her husband. She ironed and folded clothes all night, ensuring every piece was starched. Grandpa felt left out, he started staying out, making excuses for not showing up for supper.

Madea knew this type of thing could happen, especially if there was no sexual contact between the two.

"I love that damn man, but I must not have any more babies" Grandpa loved Madea; he wanted that intimacy that he thought he selfishly deserved as a man. He never imagined the negative impact it would have on his wife and family, not having the ability to control childbearing. Of course, it appeared Madea was selfish and cruel in her own way, but she knew the devastation of rearing the children and not having adequate means of support. "I want my babies to read and write and learn much more than what we had."

She also knew that the children might miss out because she and Grandpa would be working to provide for them as they would be responsible for caring for the younger ones. Grandpa accepted what Madea was feeling and decided to continue to occupy his time and talent fishing as this was a means of financial support. He engaged himself in multiple relations as this satisfied his sex drive.

He never intended to be unfaithful; he felt deprived and shut out. Although Grandpa provided food and necessities for the family, he missed some very important times spent with Madea and the children. Grandpa and Madea decided to dedicate their marriage by simply loving each other, and therefore, they started sexually embracing each other as often as two married individuals possibly could.

Little Johnny was ten months old at this time; Madea knew she would be nursing the youngster for at least two more months before he becomes weaned from her breast milk. She knew that all her dreams and desires may be forfeited because there were no contraceptives for her or her husband at this time; they had no doctor or any kind of family counseling.

Madea began to experience those nauseous mornings, those long patterns of sleep, and missed periods. Grandpa did not wake

Madea; he simply prepared the morning breakfast as Madea herself would do. Madea gently opened her eyes, sat up, and turned her small frame towards the breakfast table, grabbed her housecoat, and ran towards the slop jar behind the makeshift door.

She began to vomit profusely. Madea knew she was pregnant again. She got up from the floor and opened the makeshift door that was concealing the slop jar. She slowly walked towards the wood-burning stove where she gathered her wash water to give herself a sponge bath. Just the smell of food made her queasy.

She whispered sadly. "My Lord, I can't do this again, I won't do this again. Madea did not want any more children at this time for fear of not being able to give the three that she had a chance to be proficient. She worked all her life helping her family as a field hand, a daughter of a sharecropper, so she and her family could remain on the plantation.

The family's stay would be free as her parents shared the harvest with the owner. Madea was not able to attend school; she remained without book knowledge as a young girl. She was uninformed and uneducated. Madea's will to learn was natural. She was quick to learn, although her parents focused on feeding the family and keeping a roof over their heads; Madea wanted better for little Johnny and the girls.

She made every effort to give the children as much schooling as possible. She would salvage old books that she sneaked out of her clients' trashcan when they were not looking, clean them up, and carry them to her church. The elders would help her read, as she was a fast learner. She taught the girls as much of what she learned at the church.

"I prayed that my children have some books sense. "Madea knew it would be hard for the family to feed the children and keep them clothed. Madea feared that this would become consistent as the children got older and needed the necessities to attend school. She decided to abort the child without consenting with Grandpa. "I will take this big dose of castor oil here and put myself in this hot water tub. "Madea repeated this silly attempt to destroy the fetus but without success.

She cried not because her attempts to abort the child failed but because her love for her family was so genuine that destroying a baby would ruin her psychologically and spiritually. She accepted that she would have other children because she was a young woman who loved her husband, and there were no known contraceptives.

Grandpa was a man that worked very hard trying to meet the needs of his family. He knew Madea was pregnant again, but he swore he would always provide for them no matter how many babies were brought forth. "I a...ra are going to love all of my children and provide for them because they are my heart's desire."

Madea was only six weeks pregnant before she noticed a difference in her body; she wanted to do what was fitting in helping Grandpa harvest the crops. Despite the swelling in her hands and feet or the occasional tenderness in her breast, she wanted to do what she thought was appropriate while the children played in the fields. Madea was a very wise young woman; she knew as the pregnancy continued. Eventually, she discontinues any chores and becomes homebound until the child comes.

"There is nothing I won't do while I can assist so my children can haves' needful things." During the fieldwork, Grandpa insisted Madea stop, rest...stop and eat with the children. Being submissive to her husband, she took his advice. Along with the food, she packed the salvaged books.

The children gathered around as Madea removed the books; they enjoyed listening to the stories that she learned to read from the elders at the church. Madea did not read the way she usually talked; the children learned to read from their mother, who lacked schooling. Madea always made do with what she had; she urged her children always to listen and be good stewards over what they possess.

The children caught on well and helped each other to read and write their names. With little education and being simply illiterate, Madea was a great home-schooled instructor for her children. She made a promise that her children would all attend some school, "If I can, all my children will have good learning." When Grandpa and the plantation owner met, they settled with the day's work.

Grandpa loaded the remaining food on the mule-pulling buggy while Madea helped the children to their places as they harnessed for safety. Grandpa sorted the produce for marketing, as this was a huge asset to their finances. Madea took the remaining food canned as much as possible and prepared the rest for supper; despite his infidelity, Madea knew Grandpa was a good father and loving husband. He made sure the children had baths while Madea did the cooking.

He can tell in her movement that she needed all the help he could render because of the swelling she endured from being with a child. The family sat and began their meal. Little Johnny was finally weaned from his mother's breast milk but still needed help in pureeing his meat and vegetables.

Madea simply detested a practice her mother and grandmother did, as the young infants could not chew properly. She swore that she would never feed any of her babies out of her mouth. Madea took the spatula and mashed the food, especially for little Johnny, even if it was fried chicken.

It was early morning, Madea acquired that burst of energy. No more queasiness, or swollen ankles that bothered her, in fact, she felt like a new woman. In her second month of pregnancy, Madea had gotten over that awful early sickness. She was up preparing for the celebration of little Johnny's first birthday. He was one year old today. Madea made a yellow cake with white frosting, while Grandpa contributed to making the ice cream.

It was exciting for the two to see their only son continue the rest of his life on such a special occasion. Madea remembered the little bible that as a gift from the midwife. She opened it and there, the blue ribbon and the handwritten birthdates that read April 5, 1914, John Henry Harris II. His father gave this name to him in honor of his deceased father, the first John Henry Harris.

Little Johnny was so frisky and inquisitive that he rolled out of the little Bunkie that Grandpa made for him; he wanted to know who put the cake on the table, why it was there, and how much he could have. "Why, this is your birthday! I make this cake, especially for you." "Now, get your oatmeal breakfast first, and we're going to have a birthday lunch." This was a new thing to Little Johnny; he did not know what a birthday celebration meant.

Madea had a picture of a child in one of her salvaged books that she read to him; she showed Little Johnny the happy child in the book and his birthday celebration. "Gal, is this me?" All the children connected to their mother with the name Gal. This was from hearing Grandpa. Madea smiled at Johnny and said, "This little boy has his own birthday party, us make this party just for you too."

Madea began to show Johnny the discarded book, as there were pictures of a child celebrating a first birthday. Grandpa was in and out of the house setting up the huge block of ice and salt for the delicious homemade ice cream. He stopped, grabbed Little Johnny, and picked him up. Around and around, they went.

He loved bonding with Johnny at that very moment. This was an awesome day to celebrate his only son's first year. When Grandpa spoke, everybody listened. His voice demanded attention. "A... ra...come here, boy and taste your ice cream." The girls finally got up, hearing their father's voice, "Get your sponges and eat your oatmeal."

Madea made sure everybody had a good breakfast to start his day. Grandpa had his huge sipping mug when he drank his coffee; the children always drank freshly squeezed orange juice. The girls were much more mature than their little brother; they knew what the cake was for and were looking forward to the celebration.

This was a tradition; Madea gave each child their first year's party. "I make cakes for all of my children; this is a gift to them." Grandpa built a small playground for the children; He constructed a seesaw and a swing set. "Look, a ra outdoors, a...about done." The girls were all amazed, and Madea was just as surprised. She had no idea what was going on outside. Just as Madea said, the celebration did take place right at lunch.

"Now, where is my little birthday man?" Madea wanted little Johnny to get the first slice of his birthday cake. Grandpa took the finished homemade churned ice cream and presented it to Madea. Everyone sat and gave thanks for Little Johnny's birthday. After the birthday celebration, the children went out to play on the swing set and hand-made see-saw, but Little Johnny did not know what was going on. All he saw was the happy faces.

With the assistance of Grandpa, the little tot played on the swing set, assimilating independence when Grandpa supported him. Little Johnny played on the swing set until he became suppressed with sleep. Grandpa gave Madea the eye to say this one is out for the count. "A ra, my little man done gave out I best am putting him down for his nap."

The girls continued to play on the swing set and seesaw. They also played until they became weary and tedious and simply gave in to sleep. Madea and Grandpa brought the children up and into the shack so they would finish out their sleep. After removing their shoes, the children were finally down for a nap. Madea began to put away the cake and food with help from Grandpa.

He gently wrapped his arms around her as he was facing the back of her in a dorsal position. Madea continued to wash the plates, but without hesitation, she turned laterally to him. The two adults began their romantic interlude, kissing and embracing each other. Grandpa picked Madea up from where she stood and carried her to the bedding area. "Wow!

My man needs a little time for love. She was delighted, as she was with a child, and welcomed the idea of him wanting her. The next day, Little Johnny ran to Grandpa, aggressively manipulating his father to take him out to play.

The girls were still in bed, and Madea had not begun cooking the breakfast "just a ra one ...minute little fellow." Grandpa gathers the morning wash water for the little one and gives him a bath while Madea slowly but eagerly gets up with one hand holding the corner of her back as if she were experiencing a slight pain. She went towards the slope jar behind the makeshift door to relieve herself.

When entering the kitchen, she poured water from the wood-burning stove for a quick sponge bath and began to wash and clothe herself. As Grandpa laced the tot's boots, he noticed her movement; immediately and unselfishly, he took charge, gently pulling Madea by the hand and insisting that she remain seated in the rocker as he prepared the morning meal. "Now a... ra let us sit at the table and enjoy our blessings."

Chapter # 3

The Unexpected

After they married, Madea and Grandpa lived in the present two-room shack and started a family shortly after. The space provided the former Harris Family to live as the family occupied while they were tenants working the property as sharecroppers years in advance. Little did Grandpa know there were no documents regarding their stay when his father passed on, but he was given the word and a handshake.

The property was set up for auction immediately, and the family only had a month to relinquish the space. The news overwhelmed Madea despondently; furthermore, it caused a terrible imposition on the family, including the children.

The law saw that the family lived in the space, and no payment or tax was imposed on them. They began legal actions on behalf of the county where the Harris lived and demanded they pay restitution for their stay. Grandpa did not have the money to give regarding the matter. With little time, Grandpa remembered the business he shared with the white fellow who came in defense of the family as he consulted his lawyer.

Grandpa was illiterate, so the burden was dismissed; the obligation to pay changed to no pay during his stay. Grandpa had to uproot his family and move on. The entire work that Grandpa had done for the space and his dreams of an inheritance for his family and the children's playground was all gone. "My family a...ara will get a new home. "Madea was very sad, not because she had lost her home but because she saw the hurt in Grandpa's eyes.

"We were blessed to have the white fellow helping us; he was jest an angel," Madea reassures Grandpa that all was well, that their growing family really could use a larger space. After packing all they had on the mule and buggy, Grandpa says goodbye to the plantation and their former lives as sharecroppers. Madea was still early in her pregnancy at three months old and had the desire to continue working as she brought in laundry work to her home.

Grandpa continued to raise and sell his hogs to care for the family while Madea, and he were given another space, not permanent and not for rent, but just to live and take care of their babies as one day they would have to vacate the property when asked.

Madea knew a well-known family whom she promised to work for in their home after she delivered her baby. The family-owned the space, and just like the previous property owner, there were no written documents as to a long-term stay or ownership. There was no tax imposed on Grandpa or Madea; the property was private, and the owners prepaid the tax.

The plantation houses set above the ground constructed of framed dwellings with fireplaces and wood-burning stoves were the norm. The space was twice as large as the previous property, bearing three rooms, including a kitchen area. "If I a... ra might bring some hunting in, I could a...ra buy shoes for the family?"

Madea knew sharecropping supplied most of the monetary sales and helped with their food shortage when she would store those items for future needs, and the grains were left to feed the hogs, although Grandpa had to sell the mule and buggy to meet the need of his growing family. Madea was accepting of the idea, as she had always walked during her lifetime.

The family moved closer to other relatives. As Madea grew larger in her pregnancy, she continued to can food and salvage whatever she thought would be of use to her family; she swore her family would never be without food. "I will can all I make from my washing jobs." Of course, Madea and Grandpa had problems ahead, but these types of setbacks never stop the love they shared as a couple.

It was the middle of summer, and hunting season was ways off, but fishing was a time that Grandpa simply relaxed with his pals and collected game for the market to sell as his family depended on the extra income. Still, without intent, Grandpa became intoxicated and therefore explored multiple partners in various affairs. Grandpa always comes home to Madea, but there was an extended bloodline because of such affairs.

Madea and the children were happy to see Grandpa as the long days became overbearing as Madea had to calm the crying children and perform her home laundry without the help of her husband. When returning to his home, Grandpa brought supplies and gifts and dishonesty. He knew being unfaithful was not a characteristic the Harris possessed.

As a wife, Madea wanted to comfort and reassure Grandpa that she was a good listener and a patient wife. "Us misses you; us wants to know if you have enough food, what you ate on your fishing trips, and where you sleep. Was your fishing hard to ketch?"

Madea was curious; she felt the need to comfort Grandpa as they conversed after being apart for an extended period, and she never implied that there was anything extra-marital going on. Gal, a...ra you and the children are all I got, there a...ra ain't anything else but my family," he sought not to commit to honesty. He knew this would hurt Madea and cause great stress on his wife as she is with child.

Madea knew as she looked into his eyes that Grandpa was still hurting, but her patience and endurance of knowing that there was strong love between the two of them and that this too shall pass.

Grandpa subconsciously ignored his pain when forced to relinquish his parent's house, as he simply subterfuges the thought of expressing how uprooting from the childhood house compacted his life. He took to alcohol and outside relationships to comfort what was lost after his property auctioned; although Grandpa was secretly saddened, he discontinued his fishing trips and sought not to impose any more on Madea during the pregnancy.

It was a season of hardship, but Madea and Grandpa made every effort to make do with what they saved and what they had as the unexpected arrivals. Grandpa knew that being in the third trimester of her pregnancy, Madea needed a midwife's assistance to help with their child's birth. Finally, there were family and close acquaintances near this residence, and there was a midwife by word of mouth in the area who would come and deliver Harris's baby.

Madea was days away from her due date, as her water had broken, and she was in extreme labor pain; she needed help immediately. Surprisingly, the midwife came; not the previous one, but someone unexpected. She arrived with relatives who shared their help in this delivery.

Grandpa and the midwife knew each other from an intimate relationship they shared just months before Madea's labor. Grandpa noticed the midwife's figure; she appeared to be with a child. He knew he may have an illegitimate child soon and did not know how to assume responsibility for the child. The midwife went on with her business as she gathered the clothes and warm water, carefully and gently performed her work, as she talked Madea through the breathing exercise while Madea made a final push.

Another baby girl: just like the other babies, loud and ready to suck, she washed the child, diapered, swaddled, and laid the child in Madea's arms. Madea was tired but very thankful for what the midwife had done for her and Grandpa, asking politely and with compassion and concern as she looked towards the midwife, "When do you have your lil one?"

The midwife hesitated momentarily, "soon, very soon." Madea and Grandpa made provisions for the midwife when they saved their goods as payment for the delivery of their child. "Pleases if you will; takes the goods, that's us puts together for you." The midwife shook her head and replied, "It's okay." She did what she came to do, gave instructions,, and left. Moments after the midwife's departure, Madea's relatives who assisted her left as they were her liaisons to get help in time of such an emergency. Madea was relieved that the child had finally come but bewildered and asked Grandpa a question.

"Why does the midwife take nothing for her help?" Grandpa was in a quandary and uncertain about how to explain without being truthful about the affair he and the midwife shared. Madea called Grandpa to the bedside and handed the sleepy child to her father to lay on the cradle he built for the other siblings. He felt so unworthy of the blessings of a new baby because his deception had caught up with him. "I a...ra got something to say."

Madea looked into Grandpa's eyes, put her hands over his lips, and softly whispered, "Shush, I'ze knows all about it; us wasn't speaking a midwife with child, but I'ze can see the hurt in your eye." Madea was also hurt, but she loved Grandpa; regardless of how unfaithful he had been, she would always stand by him. "You must find your child and give your love before leaving this world."

Grandpa was speechless and did not know what to say about the affair. He thought it might be worse if he began to talk, but he also knew in his heart that he could or would not lie. "I a...ra love you, Isabella Lee Harris, forgive me."Madea, so wise and caring, thought to herself after giving up the home where Grandpa lived as a child, he did not cope well; instead, he chose friends and alcohol to deal with his stress. "I'ze knows, and I"ze do forgive you."

Grandpa did not deserve the love and devotion Madea had for him, but he never deliberately disrespected her. Madea knew Grandpa would face future temptations that were not loyal to their marriage or children, but with love in their family, he would find uncommon strength in his heart to overcome such trials. After conversing with Grandpa, Madea called the children to the cradle to peek at their baby sister.

"Here's your baby sister; take a little peek." Weak and tired from childbearing, Madea suddenly drifted off to sleep. While the children were getting acquainted with their baby sister, Grandpa silently stepped into the kitchen and began to sit at the dinner table for the little ones' meal, food Madea had previously prepared. The next day, the child and Madea were up and in the rocker as Madea breastfed the youngster.

Grandpa woke up, saw what an amazing family he has, and realizes that he may go through some difficult times but will never forget what it meant to have that warranted strength of endurance. After the infant finished nursing, Madea began burping the infant as she placed the baby over her breast. Grandpa assisted Madea with the newborn as she prepared the bath.

Madea bathed the little girl, clothed her, and then laid her face up in the cradle. Grandpa prepared breakfast while Madea took her morning bath. He made the normal meal with coffee and freshly squeezed orange juice. Grandpa prepared breakfast, especially for Madea, as the two sat and had their meal. Madea begins to reminisce about the two-room shack Grandpa lived and grew up in, and how she can help him overcome his anxieties about losing what he thought was his.

She thought that if they could talk about his pain, the self-indulging would cease. He would know that Madea is the only friend he could ever confide in because of her love and her interest in him as her husband. "My love for you is all I'ze have, and us will get through this; just let me know your thoughts; please don't shut me out."Grandpa took both of Madea's hands, put them into his, and thanked her for understanding him.

"I a...ra will n...never be such a damn fool again, a...ra my family is first in my life." As Madea and Grandpa continued to converse, little Johnny got up, still sleepy-eyed to find comfort in his mother's lap. He knew she would read and sing to him as he fell asleep. The girls got up moments after Johnny, as they knew what to do before entering the breakfast table. After they washed and dressed, they joined the adults and their brother.

The oldest child was very curious about the goods that were stored next to the pantry as she saw a beautiful handmade bow that Madea made to present to the midwife for her diligence in helping deliver the baby. Madea has always taught the children to speak like the characters in the salvaged books they read and never speak like she and their father.

"Gal, did we forget to give the lady her present? Will she come looking for her gift today? When will she come back?" Madea was impressed that the six-year-old was so observant and thoughtful that she simply decided to tell the child the truth, but to do it at a time, the child would comprehend and excuse those things as the family tried to unify their relationship.

"My precious child, I'ze going to tell you soon, but it ain't going to be today." "For now, the lady just didn't want us present." The children continued to eat their breakfast while Grandpa washed and dressed little Johnny, beckoning him to wake up for his morning meal. Madea emphasized to the girls to read every day after breakfast. "Come children, make hastes, and let us read before the baby wakes up."

The girls enjoyed reading and writing for Madea. This was the best moment of the day as they learned how to assist their father and mother in their everyday affairs. Madea took the initiative to learn to read from the church mission and turned the effort into home-schooling the girls. She promised herself that her children would have an education.

Grandpa and little Johnny finally entered the breakfast table again; the little tot was sleepy and aggravated, desiring to get back into his mother's lap to finish out his nap while the rest of the family had their class with Madea. Little Johnny began to cry and yell repeatedly as he said, "I want Gal! I want Gal!" Grandpa spoke with a convincing voice; everyone stopped and respected as if being escorted to a prison chamber.

"A...ra you...will get to the ta...ta...table now for your meal." Little Johnny, with no choice at all, obeyed his father. After the little tot had his meal, he wanted to play like any little boy. He wanted to run, climb, and stump. Madea laughed and said, "Boys will be boys." Grandpa spoke again, "A...ra quiet; don't a...ra wake the baby.

"After the girls finished their daily reading and writing, they all went outside with Grandpa to play and pick pecans as this was a special time with his children. While the baby slept, Madea took a moment to relax. She promised the property owner who owns the rent and tax-free plantation house that she would assume her responsibilities as their house cleaner as soon as she recovered from childbearing.

While the children rested, Madea made aprons and dresses for the girls when she had time. She stitched clothes and darned socks as a means of finance when there was no fieldwork for the family. Suddenly, there was a soft cry. The infant was ready to nurse, and she needed caressing because of the time she had spent sleeping.

Madea gently raised the child from the cradle and pampered her while removing the soiled clothing. She removed her breast, fed the child, and began singing a sweet lullaby, burping and cuddling the child as she bonded with her. As Madea held the child, she remembered how insensitive she was to the unborn child, the depressed state of mind she had built up, and the desire to abort the unborn fetus. She began to cry and ask for the child's blessings.

"I'm so sorry. Mama loves you so much. Please forgive your Mama." Madea decided that she would always protect her children no matter how often she conceives. She knew there might come a time when the family would go without necessities. Still, she and Grandpa will support and standby their offspring no matter what condition they may be she continues to talk to the child as if the infant knew what the adult was saying and as she continues the bonding process.

Madea kissed the child, and without holding back, the baby gently closed her eyes as to drift off to sleep. Madea laid the child's face up and kissed her forehead to say welcome. She finished her days stitching for the children, their father, and her patrons, who owed her a wage for her work.

Grandpa and the children continued their fun outside until little Johnny became restless and wanted attention. As Grandpa led the children into the house, little Johnny ran to Madea for comfort. Johnny grew to depend on Madea as Grandpa left for his long fishing trips, while she nurtured him as she played the role of mother and father.

Madea saw the disapproval on Grandpa's face as he gathered the pail and advanced to the door to collect water from the outside well. As Madea sat at the table for their late meal, she knew Grandpa wanted to confer with her concerning little Johnny. When the Family gathered, little Johnny wanted to sit next to Madea for her to assist him with his food.

After dinner, the girls began to remove the water from the wood-burning stove for their bath with the help of their father. While the girls bathed, Madea took Johnny, escorted the tot to have his bath, and dressed for bed. "A ra, my son might be spoiled I don't be liking it." Madea knew what she had to say would hurt Grandpa, but she consistently got her point out.

"Lil Johnny doesn't get to bond with you whence he needed you cause of your fishing trip. "She would also return and soothe the hurt by saying, "Just stick around, and Johnny will come to talk with you very soon." It was tough for Grandpa to stare at Madea face to face because of the embarrassment associated with the midwife as he was away when Johnny needed both his parents to learn what it was like to love a parent and desperately needed his father.

Grandpa knew he must make up for the time lost for his only son and needed Medea's help in doing so. "Gal, a...ra I love my family please a..ra give me a chance to bond with my boy." Madea had much to say but said little. Grandpa had another family who possibly needed him and the bonding of a parent in their lives.

Grandpa did not expect little Johnny to turn away from him and take to his mother. Grandpa knew he had to provide for his family, but the provision entailed being away from those he loved for days, even weeks. Seasonal hunting was the only source of work when there was no more fieldwork in the area where he and his family came to live. "I a...ra will never leave my family."

As a tenant, Grandpa asked permission from the property owner to gather the pecans as they abound within the plantation. He wanted to employ himself as he harvested the nuts for the plantation owner. Grandpa and Madea had no means of transporting their way, as they had to sell their only transportation because of uprooting from their home.

Madea was fortunate her employer provided a way to and from their home when she became their home house cleaner. When gathering the pecans, the property owner would send a hired hand to weigh and settle what he picked and sacked with Grandpa.

If he were lucky, the hired hand would drop Grandpa off at the shack after a long day's work. A relative nearby took in the children, including the baby, but the family had to rely on cow's milk when Madea's breast milk was unavailable. Half weaned at six months, the child required lots of her mother's milk. This was a challenging season for the family.

With all her wisdom, Madea made little cream cups for the infant. This would suffice until Madea could nurse the child. She pureed fruit, vegetables, and sometimes oatmeal to feed and nourish the little ones and called them a cream cup.

Her breast helped as a substitute to satisfy the infant. Madea's time with the children was Friday evening through Sunday night, when she had to start a new cycle of her absence from the family. She had to rely strongly on relatives as they watched the children. Madea would cry because she did not know how devastating an ordeal this presented.

She never thought she would have to endure a life from her children. Madea had an excellent work record; everybody knew her as a laundry girl. She was well-loved, and Madea developed a love for Mrs. and her family. She would do double work just to please the Mrs. "I'ze take these here laundry home and bring them back like new and fresh smelling."

The Mrs. saw Madea crying and thought she needed to pry a little, so she inquired presumptuously. When conversing with her, the Mrs. and her family referred to Madea as Bell, which was short for Isabella. "Bell, I noticed you have been a little sad; is it because of being away from your chullins?" "I'm fines Mrs. I want be sad no more."

"Why, Bell, just take the laundry home and do your work while you nurse them youngins." Madea began to cry again. "Ah shoot, Bell, what 's the matter now." "I loves you Mrs., you just an angel I cleans really good before I go's, and I going to come right back and check on ya'll."

"Bell, there's no need to come back, Mr. and I will deliver the laundry to you each week; just have them ready for pickup, but we have something very special to tell our employees." The Steindlers make it known to Madea that the family will be transitioning away to Alabama because this is where their son was doing his first year of law practice. "

The Mr. and I have decided to move out of Georgia due to my health and the closeness of our son, who will be helping us make good business dealings. "The Steindlers was a wealthy family. They continued to pay Madea her usual wage of five dollars and allowed her and Grandpa to remain a tenant rent-free if they desired with no contract.

"Bell, I come to know you as my special friend, and I like to think that you and your children are taken care of by offering to continue your weekly wages. The Mr. and I will be visiting because of our investments in the properties and will deliver your work on a regular basis. We also have friends whom we made known of you and your awesome work habits and sweet personality. They are also in need of a laundry girl."

When Madea returned home that Friday afternoon, she began to prepare for how she would start her laundry business. Being home with her family, she was able to care for the entire household. When Madea and the relatives congregated, Grandpa would slaughter a hog and have a family reunion. He would give the relatives goods for their help in support of babysitting their children.

Madea did needlework for the relatives as thanks for their help. There was never monetary pay, but there were precious items such as goods and physical help as they would prepare food and lend a strong back as needed. Madea continued to home-school the girls as salvaged material that came available from her job.

She was given clothes that were hand-me-downs. Madea thought this was priceless; she was able to clothe her children with warm clothes and books that they loved to read. Grandpa's contribution to the family's finances led him to work in the pecan fields daily.

Little Johnny was always curious and ask Madea, "Gal, why did you go away?" "Why did you leave me?"

"Gal, will you rub my feet? I made a hurt when you left me." "I'ze will never leave you again, I'ze will always take care of you." Little Johnny had begun to make a gradual connection with Grandpa. He saw how the girls interacted with their father, and he began to open up and confide in him.

As Madea held the baby and nursed her, it was as if Johnny had gone to a little boot camp for behavioral problems. He was very accepting of seeing the little one all cuddled in Madea's arms. After nursing the infant, Madea burped, washed the child, and prepared her for bed. She took Johnny, sat the youngster on her knee, and began to read from the salvaged book.

As she read, the tot drifted off to sleep, having all the trust and reliance that his mother would be there when he awoke. Madea laid little Johnny on the bunk and covered him with the patchwork quilt. The girls were ready for bed and waiting to read with Madea from the salvaged books.

Madea's everyday language was different from the characters in the salvaged books, and the girls often wondered if they could correct Madea and teach her how to pronounce her words like the characters in the books. Madea was a person who reasoned well when the subject was logical. Every time Madea would say, "I' ze, aint, or whys," The girls would say, "No! Gal, you suppose to say, I, it is not, I'ze, and whys.

She made a conscious effort to speak in a way that would help the children continue with reading and understand why it was important that they had an education. She was a natural and easy learner. She listened to the girls, even Little Johnny, how he learned to talk just by mimicking the girls.

Madea made sure her speech did not interfere with the children's learning. She did not expect the children to teach her how to speak properly; but she knew their performance was noticed in their speech as they were taught. Madea did not know how to read, but she schooled herself by taking up with the church mission and asking someone to help her with the salvaged material she had stolen from a trash can.

She turns this effort into a successful home school for the children. "Lord, I know your angels are watching over me and I will learn to talk right." Madea would talk in a different language with her children, so there was no confusion as they learned from the salvaged books. This was her prayer. When the children all tucked in bed, Madea began to teach the girls how to pray in the way she learned as a child herself. They repeated the prayer every night at bedtime; even Little Johnny learned how to pray with his sisters.

When the children were all nestled in their bed, Madea and Grandpa made time for each other as they intimately engaged themselves in the comfort of each other. The couple was very much in love and took advantage of every moment to make a special effort to enjoy a bit of romance as their time away from the children and each other influenced their relationship. "I a...ra missed you Gal, I a...ra never loved anybody like I a....ra love you."

Grandpa observed Madea's language as she began to speak. "I loves you so much, I cries whence my family was not with me." It was impressive; he thought it was great when her words were full sentences. Grandpa was illiterate as some thought, because he often stuttered and was slow with words.

Grandpa was much more experienced with reading than Madea. He learned to read early on from his aunt, a former slave who instilled the essence of learning in every child.

Unfortunately for Grandpa, his aunt's departure stunted the interest in an education as he had to walk miles to school as a very young child and finally to help his father with chores as they were sharecroppers. "I a...ra love how you speak, you learn well; a...ra chillins have a good teacher.

Madea was pleased and delighted to know that the family appreciated her efforts. She never had much, but she made what was available a milestone in her life. She took a little and made a lot out of it. The next day, Madea had to work to do laundry and lots of it. She was an early riser; she made every moment count. She made the breakfast for the entire family as they prepared for the day.

Grandpa continued to pick pecans and settled with the hired hand. With Johnny and the baby not yet weaned from her mother's breast, it was a challenge for Madea. She had the pots boiling bright and early. She was very much in shape. She carried the well water as it was dumped and heated into the large cast iron pots for washing. She used the bamboo sticks to remove scorching hot clothes in the cool and clean rinsing water.

Madea worked fast and ensured all clothes were taken in before night falls. Madea continued with this work order weekly as she did business at home, making things simpler than when she was with her children. The Mr. and Mrs. continued to deliver the laundry as they collected fresh clothes.

Madea would always receive a special gift. Food and clothes for the baby and the children because the family built a special relationship with Madea because of the kindness and integrity she had shown the family during her stay as their home house cleaner with chores as they were sharecroppers.

"I a...ra love how you speak. You learn well; the a...ra chillins have a good teacher. Madea was pleased and delighted to know that the family appreciated her efforts. She never had much, but she made what was available a milestone in her life. She took a little and made a lot out of it. The next day, Madea had work to do, laundry, and lots of it. She was an early riser; she made every moment count.

Chapter # 4

A Sense of Humor

It was not until late winter when the baby weaned from Madea's breast milk, and Little Johnny was soon to be two years old. The Little tot hurried to the cradle to fetch the now crawler, fiddled through the salvaged books, and began to read to the youngster; he knew that this was the normality for Madea as she read daily to all of the children.

Johnny thought if he took over and pretend to be reading, ,then Madea would not be cuddling the crying youngster and bby-passingher; instead , Grandpa saw the act and thought this was the most hilarious thing he had ever seen. Grandpa loved little Johnny so much that he did not try to chastise him or talk harshly, and he simply loved the scenery.

Little Johnny was as fast as a train when he saw his father watching him and shaking his head. "I a...ra got you now, so let's find you so...so...something in this little book to read." "Oh! a..ra can you read a...this story to me?" Little Johnny just giggled and sniggered until he completely gave in with laughter. He had so much fun with his father, and Grandpa just knew this moment with his son had finally come.

Little Johnny found a fresh and exciting, fun filling experience hanging out with someone like him, a male figure, someone whom he can crawl all over and play on the floor with. Madea heard the little tot as he screamed while playing with Grandpa. "That is enough." Madea tried hard to remember to change her language, to talk like the characters in the salvaged books; it was hard, but she made great progress.

She saw the excitement in the two and realized the day had come her prayers were answered. She was ecstatic to see Johnny open up to his father. "Well, who woke up the baby?" The little crawler stared at Grandpa and little Johnny as if in a movie theater. Madea picked up the child to bathe the little one while the two males continued with their fun time.

The girls got up from their sleep one by one as they heard the rustle and bustle and the noisy bumping about of Little Johnny and Grandpa while they played on the wooded floor. There was so much happiness and excitement in the air. The girls wanted to join in the fun before Madea stopped and said, "Girls, wash up and get ready for your meal."

They noticed the difference in the way Madea spoke her grammar and language and began to giggle because there was no shortcoming in her speech. Madea thought the girls was up for a practical joke and said, "What now, lets us make hast!" The girls continued grinning as they were delighted to hear a change in Madea's speech and proceeded in obedience.

After the two girls finished with their baths, they sat at the table for the morning meal like Madea taught them, as these were their daily chores. Grandpa and Little Johnny hurried to the breakfast table and took their places when the little tot shouted and said, "I want to sit with Papa, I want to sit with Papa." Grandpa was very emotional; it was hard to look at the family.

He was very touched. Little Johnny verbally recognized him as his father, realizing he spent the least time with his children. There was not only a family bond but a spiritual bond. Madea knew immediately what had taken place. She cried out, "Glory to God, thank You." After the morning meal, the family began their daily activities.

The girls had to read the books that the Mr. and Mrs. gave Madea. They are the family who owns the plantation and Madea's employers. The girls could teach Madea from the new books, as they could move up from where they started. Madea so wise and so accepting she knew in her heart why the girls began to grin before the breakfast started.

The girls were amazed and began noticing the change in Madea's grammar; "Gal, You talk just like the people in the salvaged books." Before learning to read with the church mission, she was aware of how peculiar her speech was. She also knew how it may affect the children's ability to learn from her. She knew this was the only way to maintain that confidence in her children's educational future.

She simply talked as she taught from salvaged books and those that her employer gave as gifts. After the day transpired, Grandpa and Madea had a moment of privacy, a time to talk. Grandpa looked at Madea, smiled, and said, "A...ra th.th...thank you Gal; Li...Li...Little Johnny a...ra accepts me, and I need him as much as he needs me."

Madea reminded Grandpa of a previous conversation when she simply said, "Jest stick round, and Little Johnny would come to take with you." Madea and Grandpa invested much time into their family, even if it meant devising a makeshift playpen so that Madea could watch the children and perform her laundry chores for the Mr. and Mrs.

She had time to read to the children between washings. Meanwhile, little Johnny had another agenda; he wanted to follow the path his father had walked hours earlier. "Where is Johnny?" Madea began to holler and scream and rant because Little Johnny was not in place; he did not answer at her call.

The girls were speechless prior to missing Little Johnny. They played with the baby near the makeshift playpen while Madea did her chores; they were to babysit both Little Johnny and the baby. They had no idea Johnny would pull a sneaky and clever stunt. The girls, nervous and afraid, thought Madea would chastise them because of their complacency as they lost watch on both children.

Madea remembered that Little Johnny wanted to follow his father as he watched Grandpa from the window as he carried his bucket and stick and disappeared through the thickness of the pecan groves. Madea took the baby and had the girls to come inside of the shack and remain inside while she located little Johnny.

She knew there were mad dogs and thought about nothing but rescuing her child. Madea went through the groves, yelling franticly, "Johnny! Johnny!" Finally, Johnny appeared with Grandpa. "A...ra I knew Little Johnny was going to a...ra try this trick one day." Madea did not know what to say; she was simply relieved.

"I just knew them mad dogs had torn my baby apart." Madea wanted to chastise the tot, but she hugged and kissed him and said, "Johnny, Momma loves you, but stay with your sisters, Momma was hurting cause I just knew them dogs come upon you, as she tried hard not to make a mistake when speaking. Grandpa purposely worked near the shack where there were bountiful harvests so he would be within walking distance.

"I a...ra saw Little Johnny just as he left the girls." This was the first real fight Grandpa and Madea had ever encountered. "Alright, Mr. Harris, Johnny is just a baby himself; he needs to know when to stay put." "Did you ever think about them damn mad dogs?" Grandpa reminded Madea that she was slightly misled and that there were no mad dogs in the area because they were on private property.

"I a...ra would a...ra never let my son get hurt, and there ain't no mad dogs in these parts. I a...ra so...so...sorry you got scared." Grandpa and Madea with Little Johnny entered the shack as the girls waited for Madea to bring home Johnny. With all the commotion, Madea was a bit behind on gathering the clothes from the outside lines. At that moment, Grandpa helped Madea with the chores as they brought the clothes from the clothesline.

Grandpa and Madea worked as a team when there were a number of projects to finish before the end of the day. Grandpa helped prepare the children's bath while Madea and the girls sat at the dinner table. After consuming the meal, Grandpa and Madea tucked all the children into bed. Madea and Grandpa continued to fold and iron the laundry as a team.

They conversed briefly about Little Johnny. They knew it was imperative that the children always remain near the shack. "Gal a...ra our little tot ain't gonna sit still; we a...ra just have to find a...ra something to keepum busy."Madea's speech has improved tremendously. She has worked hard to improve her education for herself and that of the children.

"The girls will have to keep a tight watch over Little Johnny while I work the chores." "I a...ra won't let you keep Johnny a...ra closed in; I a...ra was looking at a litter of puppies; I believe if a...ra he keep busy if he had something to a...ra...take care of.""Now where will we get a puppy that's already house-trained?" "We will a...ra...let Little Johnny a...ra work with the pup he can a...ra train the puppy as he grows.

Madea looked bewildered; she did not want to say anything to seem untrusting of Grandpa's idea; she had always given him the respect as head of the house. "Gal, I a...ra don't like that look." Madea simply sighs as if she may say something about Grandpa's idea at any moment, as it behooves her not to give her opinion. Madea's grammar and speeches can't train the tot alone.

Grandpa, looking all masculine and amazed, "That's a…ra why he a…watches me, he mimics the a…very things I do, and he does the sa…sa…same." Grandpa had his plan in motion of giving Little Johnny a birthday present: a little dog. Madea began to welcome Grandpa's idea about the puppy and his plan to train the little pet.

When reading to little Johnny, she noticed how he would point to the pictures bearing the dogs and other animals and how much fun he had when Madea made the sound when mocking the appropriate characters. "I believe you have a good plan; I think this will work; it's going to be the best gift a little boy could ever receive."As Madea and Grandpa agree, they prepare for where the little puppy can be abode.

The next day, after the morning meal, Grandpa went to the pecan field to work; during lunch; he and some of the workers stopped and advanced towards the pecan conveyor as the nuts were processed. Near the processing plant were kennels with dogs, housing a litter of pups. "A…ra you got a mighty fi…fi…fine liter of pups there; wha…wha what is your going price for the puppies?"

Grandpa's wages were nothing more than six dollars for an entire week; the hired hand asked for three dollars for the male puppies and two dollars for the female pups. Grandpa paid three dollars in advance for a male dog; he knew Johnny's birthday was coming up and asked if the pup could remain in the kennel until he made arrangements.

When Grandpa returned home, he enlightened Madea on all of his business dealings concerning the present for Little Johnny. Madea, happy and supportive of Grandpa's business dealings, was very delighted about how he included her on the gift for Little

Johnny. Trying so hard to remember to practice talking proper grammar, Madea realizes if she fumbles just once, no one will notice the mistake but herself.

"I know you thought about what I may say about the new pup, but I do think you are handling this great." For his confidence in her, Madea prepared Grandpa's favorite meal just to show that she appreciated his thoughtfulness and caring. Suppertime was when the family talked about their daily experiences and what they endured during the previous hours, whether good or bad.

When the girls began to set the table, the oldest girl revealed Little Johnny's hurt when he tumbled and scraped his arm while trying to hide from their care; Little Johnny loved to climb and play but did not realize that he may hurt himself. He knew nothing of how important it was to mine his sisters and the safety of his playtime as a little tot.

"If a...ra I ge...get some wire fe...fence and tree limbs to make Little Johnny a playground." Madea had no idea that the accident had taken place; she stood up from the table, looked at the scrape on Little Johnny's arm, and applied some ointment and a small dressing to protect the wound. She felt that she, as a mother, should have checked on the tot when she heard the excitement.

With all her motherly wisdom, she realized that Johnny might endure other complications. "We know that Little Johnny is fast, but let me know if he falls and make a hurt."Madea was just as concerned about the scrape as any mother, but she wanted Little Johnny to experience obedience, as it was time to chastise him for getting out of control.

Little Johnny was so special to Grandpa that he agreed with Madea; he didn't want anything major to complicate the little tot's life; he knew boys will be boys; but he also knew it would be better safe than sorry when protecting his son. "Johnny you a…ra a little big boy; it's time to a…play with your sisters and not a…ra alone."

Grandpa hugs and kisses Little Johnny as he talks while Little Johnny is comforted and trusts what his father says. Madea finds this session with Grandpa and Little Johnny very extraordinary; this is really parent-rearing their child and love. Madea feeds the baby girl while Little Johnny and Grandpa continue to enjoy their special moment together.

Grandpa loved all his children, but he wanted Little Johnny to be able to be protective rather than a hinder for his mother as he was the second male in the Harris family. "I want you a…ra to be a good lil' fe…fe…fella mind your sitters.

Grandpa called the girls over to the table where he and Little Johnny was seated and began to talk to all the children, including Little Johnny, and asked everyone to hug each other to make a special bond with Little Johnny as this would help him accept and appreciate their discretion.

At bedtime, Little Johnny wanted his father to read about the little animals in the salvaged books; he wanted to show Grandpa how he loved the animals and that he was one of the characters in the little book. "See Papa, this is me with my doggie; ruff, ruff, ruff; that is what Gal says ruff, ruff. Can you say ruff, ruff, and ruff?"

Grandpa looked at Little Johnny as he began to read and did not stutter once while he read to the little tot. "Ruff, ruff, ruff goes the dog." Little Johnny giggled and said, "Papa, you sound like a big dog." Little Johnny's eyes got heavy while Grandpa read, and he finally drifted off to sleep. When the children were in their beds, Grandpa and Madea took a moment for themselves; they embraced each other as if this moment would never come.

"My beloved husband, I never dreamed that this moment would come again; all we have gone through is a lasting testimony and a lesson to be learned." "I am a living witness when we hung in there. We didn't do it just for the love of our marriage but for the love of each other and the children."

"You a...ra Isabella Lee Harris are more than my lo...lo...lover; you are my pre...pre...precious friend, be...be...beautiful wife, the mother of my chil...chil...children, the one who took just a little out of a book and ta...ta...taught herself how to talk just for the sake of her children.

You are a learner; you a...taught me how to think not of myself only. You taught me what I think about affects others. You are someone I owe my life." After blowing out the lamp, Madea and Grandpa had a night of romance and sincere solicitousness. The next day, Madea started her chores early; she prepared a fantastic breakfast for Grandpa and the children.

She made meatloaf sandwiches for Grandpa's lunch and sweet treats to give out to his fellow associates and peers. Two days before Little Johnny received his birthday present, Grandpa made a small kennel to house for the pup while Little Johnny watched. He had no idea of what the space represented; he simply made use of his time helping his papa.

It was warm that April eve, just after the coolness of winter. Madea saw how the fellows were progressing and didn't need her help constructing the little kennel. She and the three girls, with a light covering about their heads and arms as the warmth of the day, may surprisingly change course at any time, took the antiqued stroller, placed the younger child inside, and went for a stroll through the pecan groves.

"I love walking with my girls. I want to tell them how proud I am of them and that God loves them, I like to teach them some of the things my mother taught me about this venture that we all are pursuing, which is life." The children were inquisitive about their grandparents, whom they never got the chance to meet. They wanted to know more about what Madea experienced when they were their age.

"Gal, did you have a little doll, and did your momma sing and read to you?" "I made all my dolls from tree branches and pieces of burlap. My momma always sang to me but was unable to read; she knew things and was very wise and smart. "She taught me how to sew and knit." "Gal, was your momma pretty like you?"

"My momma was very beautiful. She had long, soft, wavy hair just as black as midnight; she was very kind she didn't have much, but she always found something to give somebody. My daddy loved my Momma very much; he was tall and handsome. There were two siblings, my oldest sister and myself."

Madea thought if she took a moment to reflect on her life as a child, the girls would appreciate what they had, and when challenges came their way, the bond of family ties would inspire them to press on patiently. The younger of the two oldest girls was just anxious for her turn to ask a question.

"Did your big sister teach you how to read?" We did not have a mentor so my sister and I self-taught ourselves. We asked questions and looked at labeling. I owe my education to the Baptist Missionary when I was very young. They taught me from a savaged book I acquired from an abandoned box of goods holding this antiqued stroller that we are pushing.

There were other useful things. Madea was waiting for the girls to ask that very important question that helped to communicate with them and secure their educational future. "Gal, you speak just like the Momma in the salvaged books. I feel like you are a real teacher." Madea was relieved; not all her efforts were in vain. She thought to herself, "I really learned to talk properly when I worked for the Mr. and Mrs. when I did my maid work."

"Gal, you are very smart; you know everything." "Wait just one minute, young lady; I don't know everything and sometimes make mistakes, but learn from them. Just like I want you girls to do, when I was gone from you girls and your daddy to work for the Mr. and Mrs., I listened to how they talked and remembered that it sounded right. I practiced every day until I got better."

"Did she teach you how to say big words clearly?" "Sometimes, she would help me pronounce big words." "I bet she loved you because you are a good person." "Know they loved me because they are loving people; they are to me like the parents that are no longer in my life, and I will always cherish their friendship." Just as Madea thought, the weather slightly changed; it turned chilly and breezy before returning home to Grandpa and Little Johnny.

"Girls, button your sweaters and tie your scarves. We've got to be heading back to the shack." When Madea and the girls reached the shack, the little kennel put together and ready to receive the new pup. Grandpa and Little Johnny were asleep in the rocker. Madea and the girls freshened up and sat at the table for the day's last meal.

"I guess the men are going to sleep the rest of the evening." Madea went over to the rocker and gave two kisses to Little Johnny and Grandpa. Grandpa opened his eyes and said, "This one has a...ra co...co...conked out he's had his feel; he wants to be eaten no more tonight. Madea fetched the toddler's sleeping clothes; she carefully changed playwear for the bedclothes and tucked the sleepy youngster in for the night.

The rest of the family sat and ate their last meal for the day. After the family had eaten, Madea suggested that the girls take a moment to read from the salvaged books while she bathed the little crawler and got her ready for bed. The little girl fell asleep as soon as Madea laid her in the cradle. "That's a girl it's time for nightie night."

Madea and the older sibling read until each girl, one after the other, finished their bath, and both children were nestled in their beds. Grandpa was amazed by Madea's persistence in keeping the girls focused on their reading ability. "A...ra you are one that ne...ne...never stops; a...ra... the girls gonna have all they need to learn; I'm so proud that you are firm with their learning."

The pair got in bed as Grandpa blew out the lamp. It was a slightly cold April morning. Grandpa finished sipping his coffee; he grabbed his cap and winter jacket, started out to the pecan field, and began another workday. During mid-day, Grandpa went and fetched the little pup; he knew this might cause a problem for Madea because she was not used to having pets in the house, even if it is a small puppy.

When Grandpa came home, the children saw the little pup. Little Johnny was very excited; they wanted to pet the puppy, but Madea had a different idea. "I know how much your papa wants you to have this puppy for your birthday present, so we may keep him in the shack until he's a little bigger." Grandpa was overwhelmed and delighted to see such a change in Madea's attitude concerning the little dog.

Madea took an old crate that was big enough to hold the little pup, placed it inside the crate, and gave the pup water and food. "The puppy needs to be inside where we can feed him and keep him warm until he gets big." Grandpa agreed and thought he had the most sensible wife in the world." "I a...ra can se...se see how you want to help make this a good year for Little Johnny, so I will keep watch on the pup and keep him clean."

Grandpa and Madea did their part in securing a space for the little pup together. Little Johnny had no idea that he was the owner of the little pup; his birthday was a day later, and Grandpa wanted to surprise him and tell Little Johnny that the puppy was all his. After supper, the children sneaked and petted the little pup, even the little crawler.

"Okay, that's enough. Let's get to bed because we've got a lot to do tomorrow." Everyone raced and got in their beds, as they were very enthusiastic about tomorrow. "I a...ra... think everybody wants to claim the pup; there might be some fighting going on." Madea had already considered that the children must share the new pet even if it represented Little Johnny's day. "We have got to teach the children that love comes with sharing, so everyone will take time to care for and love the puppy."

Grandpa cleaned the little pup's crate the next day by removing all the waste. He fed and gave the puppy fresh water. The children heard the commotion as Grandpa tended the little dog. Everyone got up, including Little Johnny. He was excited and wanted to pet the little dog.

Grandpa took Little Johnny by the hand and said, "A...ra son, this is your birthday, and this is your present, the little dog, but we want everybody to love and share the puppy; let your sisters pet the pup and help care and train him." Grandpa knew Little Johnny was strong-willed and very aggressive, but he had no idea the two-year-old would pull a cunning stunt as the family briefly missed him.

"Johnny, Johnny, Johnny, I guess he's on the potty doing his business; he's not there, and where can that little fellow be?"

The girls looked into the little crate, and the puppy had gone. "Papa, Gal, the puppy is gone, and Johnny took him!" Madea got scared; she knew Little Johnny had gone into the thickets of the pecan grove with no secure covering about his head and arms, and he could catch his death from pneumonia.

Grandpa felt guilty; he thought this might be all his fault when he asked the little trooper to share his birthday present with the girls. Grandpa began to call out Little Johnny with his deep baritone voice. "A...ra...John Henry Harris,, where are you?" Grandpa fetched his jacket, cap, and neck scarf; he went looking for Little Johnny and the little dog.

When Grandpa stepped outside, with amazement, he saw Little Johnny and the puppy asleep inside the little kennel. He did not know what to do; he was relieved to see his son again. Grandpa simply smiled.

Chapter # 5

Tough Love

Madea laundered and did all the chores, and keeping up with Little Johnny was almost impossible. Little Johnny was very happy to have a playmate, just the two of them. He found a special friend in the little dog. "Come on, red." Little Johnny had given the dog a name all his own, just what Grandpa was waiting for. The dog was indeed a redhound dog, and Little Johnny just adored him; the dog became attached to Little Johnny, too.

After months of training the dog and getting to know him, little Johnny now have something to occupy his time and space. The entire family comes to love the dog, even Madea, and the baby girl, who is now two years old, follows her big brother as if he was an Army sergeant at a boot camp.

With the help of the older siblings, Johnny, and his baby sister are reading from the salvaged books that Madea found in an abandoned carriage along with other needful things while Madea takes care of laundry for the Mr. and Mrs. She manages the family's washings, prepares the meals, and makes an effort to continue homeschooling her children. Madea and Grandpa are at a standstill now from childbearing.

Little Johnny is very creative in his surprises; it is untimely to know what their little Johnny's next move is. Grandpa has never chastised his children, but he thinks this might be a learning experience for all especially Little Johnny. "I a...ra...want my chullins to le...le...learn respect and obey if I have to tap their behind once in a while."

Madea has always incorporated spanking the children, as she would call it love; she means a child would give the parent the utmost respect if he had proper discipline. At the age of four, the youngster was determined to have his way. Little Johnny thought he could do what the adults did without a warrant or justifying his actions because he was the only male child.

He would play in the thicket of the pecan grove as he saw his father heading out for work. Little Johnny and Red, the dog, disobeyed Madea and played out of sight. Madea had to discontinue her chores and locate Little Johnny and Little Red after she yelled for them as lunchtime was nearing. "I remember what I read from the bible when the missionaries taught me to read, "Sparing the rod and spoiling the child," I think it's time to paddle Little Johnny."

Madea brought little Johnny up to the shack and gave him his first paddle. Little Johnny screamed and stumped until he was exhausted. "Gal, why do you fight me?" "You don't love me no more." "Enough, young man; I paddle you because I love you so much and don't want anything to hurt you while you are all alone; you must mind me and Papa. "Madea went on with her chores after the children had eaten their noon meal.

Meanwhile, Little Johnny and the younger sibling drifted off to sleep. After folding the clothes and adding the lavender fragrance for the finished work for the Mr. and Mrs., Madea and the two older siblings tended to the regular chores as they laundered the family clothes and cleaned the shack until everyone was completely warn and ready to retire for a short nap.

During their nap, Madea heard Red, the little hound, barking profusely and generously, not giving in. Madea knew it was too early for Grandpa, and visitors were very rare because of their rural area. Madea peeked out of the window with great surprise it was the Mr. without the Mrs. coming to collect the laundry. "Mr. how's the Mrs.? Will she be feeling ok?" "Hi Bell the Mrs. sent something extra for you."

Madea was getting very nervous. She did not want to hear any unpleasantness. As the Mr. received the laundry and loaded the car, he turned slowly and piteously and said, she will be just fine; the Mrs. suffered a mild stroke this morning right after breakfast." I will tell the Mrs. how well your grammar has improved." Before Madea could respond, the Mr. cranked the car, and the new black Ford went out of the yard.

Madea went back into the shack with all kinds of presents, including her wages for the laundry. "I got to go see my Mrs. I believe she needs me. I need to know how she's doing." Madea could not wait until Grandpa came home. She knew he would make provisions for her to go see her friend and employer. When Grandpa came home, Madea asked in just one simple statement, "I need to see Mrs. now." Grandpa knew it must be very important.

"I a...ra will impose on my old co-worker and buddy, our ne...ne...neighbor who has a smooth riding late model T. We will leave after supper is fed." Grand knew the mule and buggy would never carry the family such an incredible distance. After the meal, Madea got the children dressed for the evening weather.

Grandpa helped Madea organize the children as they sat in the rear of the buggy. "I a...ra thank red will be coming with us." Red occupied the front area of the buggy where Madea and Grandpa sat. The mule-pulling buggy went through the pecan grove and out to the main highway.

The family had no way of informing the neighbor of using his son's vehicle because there was no available phone for the nether family's household. Grandpa knew without any doubt that his friend and pal would oblige him through this ordeal.

The neighbor had not driven in years but made time to teach Grandpa how to drive successfully during hunting trips away from their family. The automobile was the owner of his son, who was in the Army, as his father kept during his time in honoring his country. "I cannot refuse you because you are a man of your word."

"All I ask is to get them there safe." My son is away now; he would be impressed to know that such a special family and their dog is using his car. It was late that night when the family reached the Mr. and Mrs. for almost two hours. Madea got out with the assistance of Grandpa, and the children all got out, including Red, but Grandpa tied him to a massively bushy oak tree.

Madea and her family went to the back of the house after announcing themselves at the door. Madea and Grandpa, including the children, went to the back before entering the mansion.

After entering the house, Madea, Grandpa, and the children followed the housekeeper to an area past the foyer where books and all sorts of pictures lay hanging in the mist just adjacent to the family's private rooms were located just up the stairwell. Madea went up with the accompanying of the housekeeper.

As she entered the upstairs floor, there was a huge room just to the left called the master bedroom; as Madea entered the room, she noticed how pale and frail-looking the Mrs. appeared to be. Madea was happy to see her friend, yet hurt because of her frailty.

In a weak and soft voice, the Mrs. spoke genuinely and said, "Oh Bell, it's so good to see you; I knew you were going to come and take care of me."

Madea politely and without hesitation said, "Yes, mam, I'm here for whatever service I can render." "Bell!" I am so proud of you; your grammar is amazing; you are a very good listener and a fast study." "I hope that your children will find the reading material fun and educational."

"We thank you for the presents along with the books, the lollipops, the food, and the clothes. They were blessings to our family." "I brought my husband and my children with me; we borrowed the neighbor's son's automobile for our trip; I slept all the way, I am so sleepy these days; oh yes, they are downstairs in the study waiting for my return; I didn't want to tire you by having them follow me up to your room.

You know I have two very aggressive little ones and two very helpful older girls." The Mrs. was very observant and intentional; she saw something about Madea that she had not taken the time to recognize herself. "Bell, are you planning to add to your family soon, maybe a little boy or girl?"

"Oh no, Mrs., we have put our childbearing on hold. It is so costly to have a large family; too many mouths to feed, so much material to buy; I barely have the time to work and complete the chores." "Now, Belle, you know children can be a blessing to us. We must let nature have its course; Belle, don't get discouraged, but you are pregnant."

"Oh, but Mrs. my husband might not take to any more children right now." The Mrs. apprehensively said, "Your husband loves you, and those children are conceived in love, the love of two consenting adults; if you have a dozen children, always remember somehow and some way they will be fed and clothed."

The Mrs. was very modest in an effort to keep her illness from overwhelming her while Madea was visiting her. "Belle, kiss the children and remember our conversation." A nurse came to the room to administer medication to the Mrs. "Please, if I may give her this medicine, she won't be able to stand visiting any longer." Madea was nervous and anxious but said, "well, I will be coming back soon to visit."

The nurse shook her head after making eye contact with Madea. Madea knew the Mrs. might possibly have expired before the next laundry job. Madea went quietly down the stairway, not expecting anything. There was an envelope with her name on it in the housekeeper's hand. After receiving the envelope, she gathered her family and went out the back door.

When the family returned to the vehicle, they all took their places including red their dog, as they sat comfortably; the family was set to go back on the highway to their plantation. Little Johnny was very inquisitive; Gal, why are you crying?" Madea knew she had to tell her husband and children about the Mrs.'s illness, so she, undauntedly but heartbroken, began to tell Little Johnny and the family about her visit with the Mrs.

"The Mrs. is very ill and may not be around to receive our visitation." The oldest sibling was very compassionate and said, "I wanted to tell her that I loved the lollipops and to thank her for the pretty hat that she sent me; I love her." Madea just smiled and said, "I think she knows how much we all love her." As Grandpa drove the buggy, Madea softly rubbed his hand and smiled.

Grandpa had a very sensitive personality; he spoke with wisdom and contentment. "A...ra when pa...pa...passing away of others brings new birth in the mist."Madea, without question, knew that Grandpa was implying that she was with a child. After a lengthy ride, all four of the children were fast asleep, and so was Red.

It was accustomed that a Negro family driven on a highway be searched and taunted by envious gangs and police officers, given the era and the construction of the roads.

Grandpa and Madea have never owned a car but briefly had the opportunity to ride in one. Grandpa swore that each one of his children would one day own a car.

When the family reached the plantation, Madea asked Grandpa, "How long did you know?" Grandpa did not know about the pregnancy, but he knew Madea had taken to the Mrs. as a daughter, and the two were very close.

"A...ra when my papa...passed my cousin came shortly afterward and when my auntie pa...pa...passed my sister had her firstborn; these were signs of new birth arriving."It will be months before Madea has the baby, and are hoping for a miracle for the Mrs. "I know she can come out of this condition If she is surrounded around one's who really love her and would take care of her; I plan to be that one."

Little Red flew out of the car and ran towards the shack with the intention of discovering a trespasser or a wild game. Grandpa and Madea interrupted the children as they were in a deep sleep to get them into the shack. Madea softly spoke, "We're home, children; let's get out of the buggy."

They led the children safely up the steps and into the shack. Madea gathered the children's nightwear, gave the little ones a quick sponge, and put them to bed while the older siblings, the two girls, tended to their own needs; after a brief moment, all of the children were finally in bed, and continuing their sleep.

Madea and Grandpa did not have proper use of transporting themselves from their prospective employment. Still, they had a great relationship with their neighbor and could use the automobile whenever necessary. "Honey, I need to check on the Mrs. and help her overcome her illness. I need your support in getting me back and forth weekly, and oh, I almost forgot, where is the small envelope Where did I put it."

Grandpa went out the door, checked the car, and found an envelope just where he and Madea sat. "I a...ra found it just where you left it." When Madea rubbed Grandpa's hand, she must have accidentally dropped the envelope without consciously realizing what she had in her hand.

She opened the envelope and with great joy and appreciation, she was shocked to see so much money; cash given by the Mrs. and a letter attached to the money. "Oh my God, Lots of money. I've never seen so much money in my life!" Before they started to count the contents of the money, Madea stopped and began to read the letter. She read aloud, "Dear Belle, I am so sorry about not being able to ride out to the plantation to pick up the laundry;

I thought my condition would be better when it was time to collect the next week's work, but I may have to undergo therapy because I don't have the use of my hands. My condition has worsened. I asked the housekeeper to put this envelope in the laundry bag; you will find this letter when you receive the work.

Belle, this is a year's worth of laundry washing, and I hope things get better for you and the family. I might not see you, but I really want you to know how much I cherish our friendship and appreciate your loyalty. You have been more than an employee. You are like one of my own children. Always remember there is no color barrier when it comes to love and trust and certainly, when it comes to me.

If I am no longer around, I would like you and your family to continue living in the shack for as long as you live tax-free. I will leave this in writing for my husband and my children. You are indeed a wonderful mother who would do anything for the safety and love of her children."

Before Madea finished reading the letter, the paper was drenched as she cried excessively. "Please, I have got to see her before she leaves this world. I got to let her know that I love her so much, and she is going to be better." Grandpa remembered Madea's words when she told the children that the Mrs. knows we love her.

"A...ra do you re...re...remember your own words when you said she already knows about our family's love for her as you told the girls?" Grandpa also reassured Madea that the Mrs. is a fighter and she is very strong. Her family has nurses caring for her around the clock. "Gal, a...ra...I be... be...believe she will pull through; she might not be one hundred percent herself, but she will live."

The Mrs. was very generous about giving her money; this was security for Madea if there was no work for her. The money would help suffice until work becomes available. "I don't deserve this package; two hundred and fifty dollars is more money than I have ever seen.

This is more than a year's wage. The Mrs. has looked out for this family more than I have ever thought; she is a real angel and a special friend, and my heart and blessings will always be with her. "Honey, I've got to go and see her again; I don't want you to take me to the mansion, but I would like to be dropped off at the train depot. I would send a telegram to the train depot when I am ready to be picked up. I plan to go as soon as possible."

Madea made plans to visit her friend and employer; she and Grandpa discussed their decision of the responsibility of caring for the children during her absence. Grandpa would take her place, filling in on the chores and minding the children until she returned to the plantation. The next day, Madea packed everything she thought she would need for the visit.

She was early in her pregnancy. She had not experienced morning sickness yet but had some long sleep-ins. After the morning meal, the children helped Madea because they knew this was a trip without them. "Gal, how long will you stay?" Little Johnny felt a little mislaid without his mother. He does not remember being away from her for an extended period.

Madea took Little Johnny by the hand, kissed his forehead, and said, "My little darling, I am going to miss you. I will be back soon because I am going away for a little while to help a special friend. Can you help Papa mind the house? I know you will be a good little man. I will bring you a nice little present."

The other children were just as concerned; they wanted to tag along with Madea, but she simply calmed them and said, "You are too young, but one day you may have to help a friend, and the only thing on your mind will be making that person happy and contented.

Grandpa gathered Madea's luggage and loaded the buggy after the children took their places; the two adults took their seats as Little Red, their dog, sat near them once more; the family left the plantation and headed towards the highway. Little Johnny just had to say something about what was on his mind, although sad and teary-eyed, "Gal, I promise to be a good little man just for you; Red and I will take care of Papa and the girls."

The second oldest girl was the most dramatic of the four children; she made it known that she would continue to read, "Gal, I will remember to read and tell you what happened in the storybook when you come home, tell the Mrs. that I love the pink mittens and I love her; she will get better."

After hearing everybody say what was on their mind, the oldest child tried to hold back her feelings. She admitted how much she wanted to help care for the Mrs. "Gal, please tell the Mrs. that I would like to come and take care of her and please get better; I will take care of our baby sister and help Papa with the chores."

Madea was very touched when she heard the children speak while she poured out her heart as a mother leaving for the first time. "I love each of you, and I am hurting just leaving you for a short time, but I will get back soon to my babies; you all are special to me just like the Mrs., and I know you will be good children and help your father with the house chores and obey his will.

When the mule and buggy pulled into the train station and came to a halt, Grandpa helped Madea out with the luggage held in the opposite hand. She barely had time to purchase a ticket. The two hugged and kissed as Grandpa escorted Madea to the terminal. "Goodbye, my love. Please take good care of our babies. I will be in touch soon."

Grandpa returned to the buggy, and the children watched as Madea took her place in the area for colored people. The children waved and threw kisses to Madea as she threw them back. Grandpa rearranged the seating again and placed Little Johnny with red in the middle next to him.

Madea noticed as the buggy pulled off; she began to cry and silently prayed for her family's safe return to the plantation. As the train traveled, Madea had to use the toilet and asked, "Where were the johns?"

It became knowledge to her that the colored had their own toilets and the whites had their own for white only; Madea remembered one thing the Mrs. told her as she kept her head up and said, "Even if there is a difference in the color of our skin and heritage this shouldn't be a barrier because we are all one. After she had done using the john, Madea went to the far back of the passenger train and took her place in the colored quarters.

There were a lot of unchanged and meaningless laws that the Negroes had to abide by; Madea knew that the only friends she came to know that were different from her were those that she came to have a personal and caring relationship with. "I thought my life as a young girl was finally over. There are still vendettas that will never cease."It was a cool and brisk afternoon; Madea stood on the outside of the terminal waiting on a taxi to transport her to the mansion.

Finally,, a taxi stopped; no relation to her and not knowing her by her nickname; with extreme incivility, "Gal, where are you going?" He continued, "Speak up. I ain't got all night." Madea pretended to be ignorant and used poor grammar, falling back into her formal way of speaking so the taxi driver would not feel inferior and, therefore will render service to her.

"I'ze wuz going to the Steindler's Mansion off Sycamore Street next to the beautiful duck pond."The taxi driver immediately knew where she was going. "Get in the back." still rude and impolite, "You gonna be working for them rich ass Jews?" Madea all relieved that someone stopped to give her a lift. "Oh, yes, sir!" He got out, put Madea's luggage in the car trunk, and hurried to the driver's seat.

"What business does a colored gal get knowing rich folks like that?" Madea was just a little reluctant to answer the taxi driver. "They owns property where my family lives." The taxi driver did not know anything else but to display a discourteous act because this was where he came from. Tell me, gal, would you, by any chance, need to get back to that train terminal?" "Yes, sir!"

The taxi driver began to see something special about Madea as a real human being. Madea, with wisdom and discreet dealings with people of all backgrounds, simply responded, "Thanksz you kind sir; yousz a mighty fine man." The taxi driver began to pour out a brief reason for the disrespectfulness after nearing the mansion.

I had a little colored friend when I was a boy. My family came here from Russia. We did not care about being of a different race, but we simply wanted to make it because we had nothing; my papa told me never to play with the little dark one again, or he will paddle me.

Madea did not respond. She knew there was a bit of humanity in this taxi driver; otherwise, he would not have given a true description of his life.

The taxi driver began to comment with humility. "I was a bit rough with my speech back there, and yet you said nothing to defend your pride." Madea was grateful. "Youz a kindz hearted man." The taxi driver gave Madea his information to get in touch with him upon her departure from the mansion.

"Here is my number. Just call and ask for Sonny." Madea politely said; "Thanksz Mr. Sonny." They finally reached their destination at the Steindler's Mansion. The taxi driver got out in a hurry, opened the door for Madea, and said I will get your luggage for you. Madea paid the taxi driver twenty cents, including a tip for his services.

The housekeeper welcomed Madea when she walked up to the huge doorway, as she announced herself and went to the back of the house. "I come to help care for the Mrs." The doorkeeper was at awe he had never see Madea. The Steindler does not need any help right now."

Madea had no way of communicating with the family; she simply came in without any formal invitation. "I did not come for pay. I'm here to show honor and gratitude and to render any service I may aid in the recovery of my friend and employer. "State your name, and I will address you." Madea thought this was a little awkward, but out of respect, she went along with the doorkeeper's request.

"I'm Isabella Lee Harris."The doorkeeper asked Madea to remain outside until he was accepted by his employer and homeowner. When the doorkeeper came back, he was preparing an area he had designated for Madea to wait. "Come in, and we will find a place for you to sit. I think if you would, wait here in the kitchen until the nurse comes and escort you to the room."

The Mr. was not present at the time of Madea's arrival, only the Mrs. Nurse, who was in charge of the mansion and the workers. When the nurse entered the kitchen, she immediately started to talk before greeting Madea. "You may sleep in the servant's quarter until I decide what you will be doing." Madea felt somewhat ambiguous about not being able to see her friend.

"I was just wondering if I may just peek in on the Mrs. tonight before retiring for bed." Without question, the nurse asked Madea to follow her. The doorkeeper took Madea's belongings and placed them in the servant's quarter, where she will be sleeping that evening. When Madea and the nurse reached the top of the stairs, just to the left of the hallway was Mrs.'s room.

Madea was very quiet and sensitive; she did not want to disturb the Mrs, as her reason for being there was to help in the healing process and keep the Mrs. encouraged about getting healthy. As

Madea approached the Mrs. bedroom, she did not expect much as she learned that the Mrs. was incoherent; she was not able to assume the use of her left arm.

When Madea glanced at the Mrs., she turned and walked away from the bed; suddenly, the Mrs. spoke in a soft voice for a second time as before, "Belle, is that you? Come back. I want to see you." With respect and loyalty, Madea turned and went back in the direction of the bedroom. "Mrs. it's Belle, yes I come to see you and help you get better." The Mrs. was overwhelmed with joy to see her friend Belle and began to plead with her to stay.

"Belle, will you please stay a while this time, have you eaten? Oh please get Belle something to eat and bring it up now!" Madea, trying not to burden any anyone, politely said, "I will just get something to eat in the morning." The Mrs. was concerned about Madea and demanded that the nurse have someone prepare a second dinner for her guest. "How did you get her, and how long did it take? I want you to be fed now."

"Thank you, Mrs. I am famished for my lack of eating since early this morning, but I have survived before." The Mrs. went on with her instinct, "Belle, you are pregnant; you need food not only for yourself but for your baby; you want a healthy baby, don't you? Madea was happy to hear the excitement in the Mrs.'s voice; she knew her presence was partly the result of the Mrs.'s healing.

Madea ate her dinner and began to tire after a brief stay with the Mrs. "I will come back first thing in the morning to help with your bath, and I will read to you while we enjoy the morning air. The Mrs. blushed and got color back into her complexion; she was relieved Belle had returned to her.

She closed her eyes and drift off to sleep. After leaving the room, Madea quietly started down the hallway to exit the stairwell. The next day, Madea slept in; she was very tired from the train ride and unable to get up as planned. There were three knocks at the door; Madea realized she had slept past her morning with the Mrs.

She got up, rushed into the bathroom, freshened up, and dressed in her white house cleaner's uniform, and rushed upstairs to assist the Mrs. When Madea came into the room, the nurse had taken on the responsibility of caring for the Mrs. Madea casually spoke; "Good morning Mrs. and good morning nurse; please may I help?"

The nurse was very stern; "you may kindly take the dirty garments and do your tub washing today." The Mrs. was in and out of sleep; the medication was a bit strong, and the nurse advised Madea to complete the chores as the Mrs. slept. Madea was obedient; she took all laundry washings and did her chores as assigned."

After the ironing and folding, Madea returned to the Mrs.'s room to aid her in whatever she desired. "Mrs, I would like to enjoy this moment with you. What would you like to do? "Belle, I like to hear you read; please read to me; and one more thing, as long as you are my guest, I want you to dress in regular clothes." Without any thought, Belle took the book and began to read.

"Oh Belle you are a wonderful reader. I am proud of your accomplishments." With the doorkeeper's assistance, Belle could take the Mrs out of the room and into the study. "Belle, I got something very important to tell you, and you must listen; I know you will be leaving soon to be with your family, and you will be having the baby when you go home."

Belle knew this was a moment of intent an urgent situation. "By the time you have the baby, I may be already gone or there before; I am unable to lift my hands. They are weakening daily; my illness

78

is terminal, and I've been given morphine for my comfort, so take this moment and just let me enjoy you as my friend. Madea did not question the Mrs; she simply had a desire to make her happy with every moment she had with her.

The Mrs. began to talk about her life as a child. "Belle, you have a gift, something most of us don't realize how valuable it is to just listen. "I was not very nice to you when we met, and as a child, I had to escape horrible plateaus of life just to stay alive. However, your personality impressed me and made me realize that I, being of Jewish decent was in no way better off than you are.

The non-Jewish society do not care for me and my family for several reasons; the only thing that keeps me in their society is that I am wealthy and can make money, as we are taught. You Belle listen, and when you deliver your speech is so unforgettable it makes even the highest of esteemed consider your presence."

Madea was very sad, but she knew she had to be emotionally strong and understanding to help in the comfort of her friend. The Mrs. begins to get tired, but she enjoys her time with Belle and reminisces about her childhood life. Madea called for the doorkeeper to help get Mrs. to her room. When they reached the bedroom, Madea began softly praying.

The nurse came into the Mrs room to administer her meds and vital signs and asked Madea to step out. Madea knew the nurse was the professional one as she gave the nurse the utmost respect. She went about performing her chores, trying to appease the nurse in an attempt to keep peace flowing among the two.

When Madea left the room, she hurried outside and began to cry, "I know we are going to bring good health back into the Mrs life." Each day the Mrs. counted on Madea's presence; she felt strength through all the pain because she knew Madea cared. After days spent with the Mrs Madea, she made plans to travel back to her family.

"Mrs, I promise we will be bringing the new baby back so you can bless our child as you will be extending your hands to receive the child; you will be healthy again."

Madea packed her belongings and ate her last meal with her friend the Mrs. She remembered the number the taxi driver gave her upon heading back to the train terminal. After calling the taxi driver, Madea left the mansion by exiting the back door.

When she went to the front of the house, the taxi driver was patiently waiting to assist her in placing the luggage into the trunk. Madea did not want to turn around because seeing the mansion made her realize she was leaving a part of her family, a true friend and confidant.

She was heartbroken and withdrawn, torn between the thought of leaving an ill friend and being the wife and mother that she desperately and submissively needed to be with no compromising; she began to say to herself, "Isabella Lee Harris, you have got to press on and be faithful, those things you desire will come."

When the driver got into the taxi, he knew that something was different about the woman he previously delivered to the Steindler's mansion. She appeared to be hurting and in despair. Without hesitation and being sensitive for Madea, the taxi driver asked, "What did those Jews say to you, did somebody die?"

Madea simply shook her head and said, "My very special friend is dreadfully ill, and I have to travel back home to be with my husband and children." Madea could not finish her conversation without sobbing; she needed that moment to talk with someone other than a family member.

"Oh Mr. Sonny please forgive me I got a little carried away. Did you have a nice ride up this way?" The driver looked at Madea as she had grown in size due to being with a child and opinionated. "You should be concerned about your own, the one that is growing inside of your belly, because the health of what's not here should be your first concern."

Madea knew the taxi driver was right but wanted somebody to feel her pain in both situations. "Thanks, Mr. Sonny, for a listening ear." The taxi driver began to tell Madea about a similar situation that he had to endure before losing his wife. "My wife who is not with me had lung cancer, I thought I would die when her condition worsened, but she reminded me of how much the children needed me.

Madea was sympathetic and again asked to overlook her for being overbearing. The taxi driver went on and said, "Oh yes, there is more; your friend and employer want the same for you." It was only minutes before entering the terminal when Madea told the driver how much he helped her relieve her aching heart. "You are a great man, with a genuine heart; I feel more at ease now." The taxi driver noticed Madea's grammar had changed drastically. She did not have that shyness about herself; she seemed to have complete confidence in what she said. "Pardon me for saying this, but your language is far different than what I remembered when you first spoke to me." Madea began to laugh and said, "It is a long story. Maybe one day we will meet again, and I will tell you all about my effort in speaking properly."

The taxi pulled up to the terminal, the driver got out, opened the trunk, handed the luggage to Madea, and said, "I hope it will be very soon." After paying the driver, Madea had a special gift to give the driver. "Mr. Sonny, I made this for you, and thanks for everything." The driver tilted his cap and said, "Thank you, mam."

Chapter # 6

Returning Home

Madea prepared for the telegram that she would be sending Grandpa regarding her continued stay or departure from the mansion. The telegram would tell whether she would be arriving that same day or if she would remain until further notice. Grandpa prepared supper for the children early that evening to fill their stomachs when they sat out to receive Madea from the terminal.

He was to check the terminal, as there was no way of communicating because their family simply lived on things of extreme need. The plantation homes were not equipped with electrical services or indoor plumbing. With the use of the neighbor's mule and buggy Grandpa, the children left the plantation shortly after the last meal as instructed by Madea to receive her telegram. Little Johnny was curious as to how long Madea was gone.

"Papa, Gal was gone too long. Are we going to go and fetch her tonight? She needs to come home now!" Grandpa, with stern wit simply said, "Be a...ra...pa...pa...patient son." When Grandpa reached the terminal, he drove the mule and buggy into a safe place and told the children to remain intact until he finishes his business inside.

When Grandpa came up to the counter, he asked the attendant on duty if there was a telegram from his wife, Isabella Harris. "A...ra is this where I pick up a te...te...telegram? The attendant was disrespectful and pushy that night. "Yea boy, do I need to read it to you?" Grandpa was very polite and said, "No sir...thanks." He took the telegram, read it, and rushed to the buggy to get his children.

"Come chi...chil...children, we're just in time. The passenger train came rushing in, blowing and letting out steam.

Little Johnny hollered out, "I see Gal!" Grandpa and the children just sat in the colored folk's quarters of the station as they waited for the final stop, as the people came through assisting their loved ones while they got off the train. The train portal gave Madea her luggage prior to entering the colored quarters. Little Johnny ran to Madea and said, "I saw you just now." Madea hugged and kissed little Johnny.

"I am happy to see all of you." Grandpa and Madea kissed while he held the baby girl. The oldest two just grinned at the romantic sight. When Madea glanced at the giggling girls, she said, "Come here, you two; I've got something for you." Madea could not wait before returning to the plantation. "I've got presents for everyone!" There were boots for all the girls, a special little toy soldier for Johnny, and a tobacco pipe for Grandpa.

Everybody took their gift and exited the train terminal. When the family reached the buggy, each child took their usual place in the buggy. Johnny was so excited about his new toy soldier he would pretend to be the soldier by throwing his voice as a ventriloquist all the way home. The girls were also so intrigued about their gifts that they made plans to wear their boots to their new school and church on Sundays.

Madea was so tired from the train ride that she simply slept all the way to the plantation. When the mule came to a halt, Madea was awakened, shaken, and crying, trying to sustain herself as if she was experiencing a sad dream. "Gal, what is it a...ra...you are sweating; come inside, and I will fe...fe fetch some warm tea for you." The children got out of the buggy and helped their father prepare the way for Madea.

Little Johnny was so protective of his mother that he wanted to take on whomever was hurting her. "Gal, someone hurt you, and I am going to hurt them." Madea was delighted for all the attention that she had created, but there was no better time to tell the family about the visit with her friend the Mrs., and her condition. "My visit with the Mrs. was a lovely stay, but she is very ill, and some think she wants be around to see our new baby."

"I am faithful, and I need the support of each of you; we will continue serving the Mr. and Mrs. as often as possible." The girls were so hospitable they wanted Madea to see how much they had matured; they prepared a place setting just for Madea, "Gal, would you be having tea or milk with your supper? Madea was amazed; it was like overnight when the girls were into dolls and hand-clapping games.

Now look at my smart little ladies; did you cook the dinner too?" The dramatic one that is next to the oldest; "yes, gal, with just a little help from Papa." While Madea was having her meal, the girls washed and dressed the younger sister for bed as they did when she was away visiting the Mrs. "Thanks, girls, I'll just read her a story while you prepare your baths."

Little Johnny was still playing soldier with his little gift. Madea spoke firmly as she opened the book. "Johnny, bedtime; let's put toys away." After the family settled down for bed, Madea and Grandpa had their private moment of love and simply talked about their children's future. Madea knew she had to let the children learn outside of the home and meet other school-age children, learn different crafts, and take on activities that would prepare them for days to come.

"Honey, I think we should take the children down to the school so they will continue their learning." "The bigger children can help

Johnny learn as they are taught." "I a...ra...was th...thinking the same thing. The school is only two miles past the church." The next day, Madea took the girls out for a walk through the pecan grove and down past the church as she prepared them for their walk each day to the center for learning.

"I want you girls to attend school on Monday, please remember to take notice of our steps so you may come on your own. Madea, in her fourth month with a child, had great intentions of educating all her children. "You will start out with Papa when he goes to work in the field each day." When Madea and the girls headed back to the shack, the younger girl spoke enthusiastically as if the moment she had waited for had suddenly come.

"Gal, will I wear my new boots and scarf that the Mrs. gave me for my present?" The oldest girl saved her coins so she may buy chalk and a tablet for class. Gal, can we stop and get some markings and tablets for writing? Madea was simply delighted to know that the girls were ready to take that next step in their lives. "Oh yes, yes, yes, yes!" She was so happy about the children's desire to learn more she stopped at the corner store to purchase school supplies for the girls' first day at school.

When the three entered the store, the clerk was not welcoming and made degrading remarks about their learning abilities. "You coming in, gal, you and them youngins." Madea was as polite as possible; she always says niceness makes even the worst animal appreciate you. She used the grammar that she had before learning to read so she may appease the store clerk.

"Good morning sir, yes sir us a cumin in to git marking fur learnin." The clerk went on with his senseless attitude. "I damn shorely don't know what that gonna be; all you coloruds kin du is manage the field." Madea and the girls gathered all the supplies they needed paid the store clerk and bid him good day and started out. "Wait a minet gal; take some licorice for free for dem youngins.

Madea appreciated the store clerk's effort to overcome his ignorance. "Whys thanks sir."Madea and the girls got their candy, plus enough for Little Johnny and the younger girl, and exited the store. When Madea and the girls started out to the plantation, she knew her children would face challenges while getting an education. Grandpa did not have access to the mule and buggy daily, but he was able to walk with the girls in the early mornings.

"I said I don't a...ra want no mess; I a...ra will pro...pro...protect my family." Madea knew the girls had to branch out on their own; this was learning material for Little Johnny, whatever he see the bigger children act on, and so would he." The girls were very excited about school, so was Little Johnny. "I will keep bad people away from my sisters, me and red."

"I am ready to start." Madea was so pleased about Johnny's enormous protection for his family, but he was not quite ready to start school. "Johnny, do you remember when you were a little tot and I spanked you for the first time?" Johnny did not remember. "Ah, no, mam." Madea wanted to remind Johnny of how protective she had been of him and the girls when they were younger.

"Well, I spanked you because there were dangers around us, and you disobeyed me when I said do not leave the yard." Johnny still did not remember. "I see how you love your sisters and want to protect them; that's good! Now I paddled you because I love you and didn't want any bad thing come of you." I promise, Gal, I won't be misbehaving no more. "Gal, I had a dream last night. It was a bad dream." Madea was very concerned; tell me, my darling, what was it about?"

Johnny was afraid to talk about his dream, but he knew his parents would always protect him. "There were some men who came and shot up our house and killed everybody but me." Grandpa was perturbed about what he heard Johnny say about the dream. "Well, a...ra son, was there more to your dre...dre...dream?" Little Johnny was even more frightened about revealing the rest of his dream.

"The men came for me, took me away, whipped me, and made me work hard very hard."Little Johnny was traumatic. Madea did not understand how to deal with such an issue. She took Little Johnny, held him in her arms, and said, "My little darling, Papa and I will never leave you. We will always protect you and your sisters. Grandpa had an unction to tell little Johnny about a true experience he had when he was a boy.

"A...ra...son you will be dre...dre...dreaming more bad dreams but re...re...remember they are not real you cannot die or get hurt by dre...dre...dreaming. "Gal, I don't need to be a big boy right now, I can wait; can I sleep with you and Papa tonight?" "John Henry Harris, you may sleep with me and your Papa just tonight." The next day, Little Johnny and Red stayed close to the shack while Madea wash the laundry.

Little Johnny was still shaken from the dream. He kept red his pet, the hound dog, by his side all day and began to talk to his friend. "Red, if I die, will you come with me? You are my very best friend in the whole wide world. I know you will protect me and keep bad men away from taking me, and I know if I am asleep, you will wake me to let me know if someone is waiting to take me away.

Red, will you keep the bad men from hurting my Papa and Gal and my little baby sister and my two big sisters?" Madea prepared a snack for Little Johnny and Red his friend while the younger sibling was quietly asleep. Meanwhile, she began to wonder why Little Johnny was so quiet and not bothersome, and she called out Little Johnny's name. "Johnny! Come right now, I got a little lunch for you."

Little Johnny and his little red dog were fast asleep. "Not now, my darling. You must get a bite to eat before you nap." When Madea tried to move Little Johnny, he started to cry out, as if someone was taking him. He was indeed startled because of the abrupt touch of his mother's hand. Gal! Ga! It was real; they took me, made me work, and hit me."

Madea took Little Johnny once more into her arms and said, "there is nothing I want to do to protect my children because I love you. Please, Johnny, remember these words: even if you are bound to troubles, I will come for you. This is what mothers do, they protect their babies; there is nothing a mother wants do for the safety of her children."

Little Johnny found a sense of peace when he heard his mother's voice, and Madea could see the acceptance in Little Johnny's eyes. "Gal, I will be your little man. I will protect you, Papa, and my sisters one day. I am not afraid anymore." "Johnny, I want you to understand that you are going to have other dreams that are hurtful, but remember, sometimes they teach us, and sometimes they warn us, but in the end, there is no real harm in dreaming."

After Madea finished comforting Little Johnny,, she led the sleepy youngster into the shack. Little Johnny was simply too tired to eat. It was getting late, and the girls had yet to come in from school. After the children were quieted down for a nap, Madea began to look out for the school-aged girls, knowing they were miles away from the shack, as there may be potential harm in their mist.

Finally, there they were, including Grandpa, coming through the pecan grove. When the family all congregated, Madea began to ask questions, seeing that Grandpa escorted the girls home. "I felt relieved to see the girls with you coming in from school."Grandpa had the same idea; he wanted their time in learning to be safe and exciting.

"I a...ra went on my lunch and waited around for the girls to come out so we would walk together. Grandpa thought that, given time, the young girls would build up the security and maturity that would help them overcome their inferiority complex. "I know we have a...ra kept the girls under our wa...wa watchful eyes since they were babies; now, after traveling to and from the school, these girls are going to have the courage they need to endure any future trial in their path of life.

Madea was thinking on the same line her thoughts are more with an association, as the children will have the experience in learning what others who have come along as teachers, lawyers, and doctors. "I hope what we have given our children, they would take heed to it, make the most of what's ahead. There was a laugh coming from the children's room. It was Little Johnny.

"Now, what is Johnny's up to; he sounds very happy. I can tell that he has overcome some of his fears of napping along." Madea started toward the youngsters' room before Grandpa said, "Gal, le...le...leave him alone; he'll be just fine." Little Johnny was back to pulling his little sister's hair and teasing her. He was just full of life. "All right now, that is enough; what's going on here."

Madea was curious. "Gal, I had a good dream. We had five more girls and no boys. I had to keep all of them while you and Papa worked the field." Madea remembered what the Mrs. said about the children she will have, and now Little Johnny has the same dream very peculiar."Johnny, will you tell me more about your dream?" "No more, I can't remember." Madea was a little puzzled, "I work for the Mrs. she will be getting better soon, and I know she has to."

After weeks of schooling, the girls were able to walk confidently to and from school without Grandpa's assistance. "Madea was close to her due date for delivering the baby, and Grandpa told relatives and friends that he needed the support of all available.

Now that the girls were able to attend school without the assistance of Grandpa, he was able to devote his time with Madea during her last weeks with the child. "I a..ra will be sp...sp spending time with you while we await the little one because you need to be at rest starting today." Madea thought this was a wonderful idea; the family grew closer as they grew bigger.

"The gift that the Mrs. gave us would help at this time while I deliver the child; I'm so happy that you made this decision. It has been hard due to all the extra chores coming from the laundry; thank you so much, my darling husband. The money has also given you a breathing space away from the field. I often wonder if she knew what the outcome of what was to happen to us without either of us working during my time of childbearing;

God has given me such a special friend. I will always cherish the friendship that Mrs. and I have. "Gal, a...ra you are quite a fri...frifriend yourself, that is why so many adore you; and you have a special task when you a...pa approaches even the nicest to the meanest person in the world. I will do something special for you; we will visit the Mrs. once more before you deliver." Madea began to cry and sob,

"This was in my spirit to do, the Mrs. is constantly on my mind, and I have got to check on her; I thank you for this lovely gift. Grandpa wanted to leave for the trip as early as possible because

Madea's condition was very delicate, "We shall leave shortly after the girls reach the shack and have their evening meal." Madea knew this would be a longer ride than the train ride.

The family has several stops when driving the mule and buggy, but the expenses are economical and fit into their budget. Johnny and his little sister was playing and teasing each other as usual, when Little Johnny spoke abruptly, "the Mrs. is gone, she has gone home, and we cannot see her no more." Madea was amazed when she heard Little Johnny; she wonders why he said such a thing, as there was no close association between the Mrs. and Little Johnny.

"Johnny", Madea called softly once more, "Johnny", the Mrs. is already home now; she is at her house with her family." Little Johnny was more precise in his conversation with Madea, speaking directly to her. "Gal, you know what I mean." By this time, Madea had grown very anxious about the seemingly premonition that Little Johnny had made her aware of.

"Johnny have you had another dream today." Little Johnny answered precociously, "No, mam." this was a relief for Madea; she was not ready for any more sad dreams. Madea began to whisper to herself, "I must stay faithful and know she will be waiting for my return." As Madea prepared the table for the late meal, she called the children to wash up quickly because the family would start out soon to the Mrs.

Little Johnny had gotten quiet from the norm; he began to play with his toy soldier, while throwing his voice as a ventriloquist. "We will take the dead lady to the grave." Madea spoke not accepting precariously. "Johnny you must not talk in that fashion. Please put your toy away. No one will be going to a grave." Johnny went on and admitted his dream about the Mrs. as he forgot the conclusion of his dream. "Gal you told me that there will be sad dreams and happy ones. I did not tell you the sad part of my dream because you might cry."

At this point, Madea does not want to hear the rest of the dream. "Gal, may I tell you now, because I remember, It is about the Mrs., she was asking for you to come before she goes home."Madea pretended not to take in account of dreams and intuitions; she simply based her life on faith. "Johnny please hurry son, and finish your meal; we have a long ride ahead.

Little Johnny noticed all the commotions, the renting and ranting, and asked, "Will we be visiting the Mrs. again?" without visible emotions, Madea said, "Yes." Grandpa went out to the buggy and packed all the needed items that Madea specified for their trip. He made known to everybody that they should hurry. "Gal, children, a...ra come on." The family got into the borrowed mule-pulling buggy, and off they went again down the highway.

Grandpa had an urgent need again to impose on his neighbor's vehicle. Madea made provisions for food and rest for the family. She prepared all kinds of treats for the children and made special sandwiches for Grandpa. Grandpa had to do all the driving because Madea was far along in her pregnancy with only weeks before giving birth. "Gal, I a...ra will I be pu...pu...pulling Into that gas station for a spell so I might get a snooze."

Madea took the children through the thickets of the woods to relieve themselves because there were no colored toilets on the highway. Grandpa and Little Johnny were sound asleep when Madea and the girls returned after their personal needs were satisfied. Madea knew that they were close to the Mrs. because she had traveled the road many times, even as a child.

The children, especially the girls, began to complain and were frightened because of the stillness in the darkness; it was very calm and serene but too leery. The oldest of the siblings said nervously, "Gal, we're scared; please wake up Papa. Can we just go?" Madea felt their emotions but knew that Grandpa had to rest; she felt the need to comfort the children in a way they would understand and lose their own selfish needs.

"My darlings, you know that Papa and I love you very much, and there is nothing we want to do protect you. Now, I want each of you to touch my belly and feel the life there. Please realize that Papa and I know what we are doing. We will never put the new baby in harm's way. That said, we will protect all of you from the least of you to the greatest of you."

Johnny was asleep beside Grandpa when all conversations had taken place. Wow, what a relief for Madea; she did not have to explain too much that before getting the girls settled. After over an hour, Grandpa began to yawn as if waking up from a long winter hibernation. Madea took a cup from the packing and the still-warm coffee and gave Grandpa a nice brewed cup.

"It is first light; we can see the gold in the trees. Would anyone care for some breakfast?"Madea blessed the food, and they all ate the family's early meal. After consuming the meal, Grandpa beckoned the family to get into their prospective places in the car. "I suspect a…ra we be making a move so we may beat the rain that is in the air. Grandpa cranked the car and went full speed down the highway.

When the family reached the Alabama state line, Phoenix City the girls began to clap because this was a memorable trip. "We have only about thirty minutes before reaching the Steindler's Mansion." There was relief in Madea's voice, completely stress-free. Finally, she gets a chance to visit her ill friend. It was early noon when the family pulled into the beautiful manicured lawn where the huge mansion stood.

The car stopped, and everyone got out and stretched, including Madea and the younger sibling. Madea went to the back of the house as usual and announced herself so the housekeeper would escort her and the family into the house. The housekeeper announced Madea as she got a great reception from the Mr. "Good afternoon Mr., "Oh Belle we are happy you could come, and in the condition that you are was such a risk for you."

I am arriving with my family and would like to bring them around if it is all right."The Mr. was just as friendly as the Mrs. He insisted that the family come through the front door because the Mrs. would not have it any other way. Madea stood at the front entrance as the housekeeper welcomed Grandpa and the children into the mansion. Everyone came in one after the other and followed the housekeeper to a quiet study while Madea visited the Mrs.

The Mr. made known to Madea that the Mrs. needed her and was waiting for her return. He also explained that the disease had worsened and she could go anytime. "The doctor insists that the immediate family is allowed to visit her. "Belle you are one of the family and the Mrs. want to see you now." Madea was heartbroken but relieved she was able to see her friend before she actually expired.

"Hello my sweet Belle, you come such a long way on the buggy." Her voice was so weak there were shortness of breath as she spoke. "We want you to bring your family up to the dining hall to be feed; the cook will assist you shortly." Madea saw how thin and frail the Mrs. had become, but she managed to hide her emotions.

"Mrs., you are constantly on my mind. I want more for you; you are more than my employer and friend. You're just like a mother, a sincere angel." As Madea held Mrs.'s hand, the touch was cold and clammy, and her body temperature dropped. "I want you to beware of strangers exploiting your children, always take precautions, and protect the safety of your children even if you have to do it alone.

Madea kissed the Mrs. hand and said, "I will get the Mr. to come in as we settle my family." Madea rushed out and got the Mr. and the nurse; the Mrs. eyes were still when the Mr. and the nurse entered the room, the Mrs. died thereafter. The time of death soon came to Mrs. Eleanor Steindler at twelve noon, July 1, 1912. The housekeeper escorted the family to the dining room to eat as instructed by the Mrs.

Madea knew that this trip is the last time ever to see her friend. She knew Mrs. Steindler has deceased; she is now in heaven and her compelling desire to see her again to talk to her took place. The family was hungry and tired, even Red their dog. After the Mrs. Was pronounced dead, the Mr. came out to join Madea and the family. He did not say anything, but Madea knew; they simply gave thanks in her honor.

When the meal was consumed, Mr. Steindler took Madea by the hand and said, "She is gone, my dear Nora." Her name was short for Eleanor. "Belle the Mrs. had another request for you and the family, and that is to rest awhile before taking that long trip back to Georgia." The housekeeper escorted the family to the servant's quarters for their overnight stay.

Mr. Steindler stopped Madea and said "Belle, she loved you very much, and thanks for coming." Madea was touched, trying to hold back her emotions. She simply sobbed uncontrollably. Madea was very appreciative; she turned and said, "I will always treasure you and the Mrs.; we will leave shortly after day breaks in the morning."

Madea remembered Little Johnny's dream days before the visit; when he saw the undertaker hauling the dead woman out, she whispered to Grandpa. "I hope we miss the coming in for the body, as this may sit Johnny back." The next day, the family left the mansion after Madea and Grandpa gave the Mr. their blessings.

Chapter # 7

A Perfect Angel

As Madea and the family entered the county of Dougherty, she smiled and said, "This is where I met my friend the Mrs.; I like to remember her as we gathered together. May you sleep in peace, my loving friend."Madea and Grandpa knew that without the support of the Steindler, there will be some hard times ahead. Mr. Steindler was the backbone of the relation between the Mrs. and Madea when he simply intervenes after his wife Eleanor wants to dismiss the use of a laundry girl to their employment.

"I will go home now and have the baby. This child reminds me of a beginning relationship, a wonderful friendship, an affair, something that is going to be in my life as long as I live. The friendship we acquired when I asked for work as the Mrs. did not want or thought she needed my help. She was shrewd from the beginning, but Mr. Steindler reminded her of how a laundry girl benefits the workload of the other workers.

"After a brief house cleaner, the Mrs. and I became close, and our relationship grew. The Mrs. found in me what I knew from the beginning, whom she was a confidant, a special friend. She secretly shared some very personal and intimate family business with me about the Mr., whom she calls Max, short for Maxwell. When he was younger, he had a debilitating disease that distorted some memory.

Madea was right; Mr. Steindler was not able to make sound decisions. She was the one who hired all of their help and contributed to pertinent business affairs. He turned all the decision-making over to his son after the Mrs. became ill. Grandpa appreciated the Steindlers for their support. They provided a roof over his family's head and a job for himself and Madea.

"I a...ra suspect old man Steindler will sell the property since the Mrs. is gone." When Grandpa reached the plantation, he remembered something. "When they a...ra ...came for my family to give up our home, we could not fight for what was ours. There were no papers regarding a given promise between my father and the owner". "Yes darling, this is true, but we've been given a warranted gift from a reputable family, a place to raise our babies and work on their property indefinitely.

I believe this day was also to come, unfortunately in death. The Steindler's would never cease on their promise. They instill the same value in their son as they had among themselves." She also reminds Grandpa about her part in the agreement with the Steindler's. "As long as I can, I will serve them and their friends as a laundry maid and show them that same mercy they had for me when we confided in about the displacement of our home as we hoped for one of their plantation houses."

She simply sold herself by saying that she was a laundry girl and a tailor. The family drove up to Grandpa's friend and neighbor's house to exchange vehicle for the buggy once more. Grandpa gave his thanks again. The family seated themselves again in the buggy and returned home. "Careful a...ra, just let me take hold of your hand. Madea took Grandpa's hand and slowly stepped to the ground.

The children were all hungry again, especially Little Johnny. "Papa, I want to eat. I can eat a whole hog." Johnny got out of the buggy and ran up to the porch with Red, his hound dog, right at his side. Red has always gone on trips with the family, especially if it is an overnight stay. Grandpa and Little Johnny had to complete all chores; the animals was left at the plantation needed tender loving care upon arrival of the family.

"A...ra come Johnny lets water the trough and feed the chickens while the girls help prepare the meal. The youngest sibling wanted her toys; she missed playing with the little treasure the Steindler's gave her for birthdays. "I want my baby doll and my little tea set." Madea spoke forcefully, saying, "Now put them away, and let's wash up for now." After traveling all day, the family ate and turned in for an early evening rest.

Madea slept in and grew very tired from traveling in the late month of her pregnancy. The girls prepared the morning meal as they watched Madea early on. "Gal, we have biscuits and may haul jelly, some hog jowl, and some fresh juice." Grandpa left early, as the girls did not have school. Grandpa would not wake Madea; he grabbed his coffee and lunch and left for work.

"Where is your Papa?" Grandpa left specific instructions for the oldest siblings to take care of the chores. "He left for work, and we will wait on you while you rest." Madea knew her time with the child could be any time; she was very concerned about having a healthy delivery, so she remained relaxed. Johnny and the younger sibling sat at the table, enjoying oatmeal and juice.

Johnny was happy and ready to share his latest dream with Madea. "Gal, I had another dream last night. The angel said I would be fine and not to worry. Can you tell me what she means by this? She said I was a good boy; she was very pretty." "Johnny, I got something to tell you and the girls." Little Johnny stopped Madea and said, "Gal I know that the Mrs. is sleeping with the angels; she told me so.

I will not be afraid anymore. I am a big boy." Madea was relieved; she did not expect the children to be so strong after the loss of their friend the Mrs. "Well, son you have answered your own questions; she is your perfect angel. She wants you to know that you have a guiding angel." She will watch over you even if Papa and I are not around. The oldest siblings fell to Madea's knees and said,

"Gal, we knew something was going on, but did she actually die? Madea and Grandpa were secretive because of Little Johnny. They did not want him to become discouraged and afraid. Madea had no idea that this was such an intimate ordeal for the other siblings regarding Mrs. Steindler's death. "Oh, my dear girls, please forgive me. I should have quietly informed you.

This was due to Johnny's recent nightmares and self-confidence." The girls began to cry and sob, reminiscing about the beautiful gifts they received from the Mrs. and how her passing away hurt them. "Gal, I wrote a poem especially for the Mrs. because I knew she was very ill. I did not know she would be leaving us so soon." The younger sibling next to the oldest, the dramatic one, asked Madea if she could recite her poem.

"You are far away from me in mile, but when I close my eyes, I can see your smile. When I wrap your love around my heart, those miles are just minutes apart. I like to come and soothe your ailment, just like the nurses in the salvaged books they made well their patient. Mrs., you are the ballerina in my dream, who comforts me with the fine presents you gave me and allured my highest esteem.

I'm told that we are of a different culture and race, but you to me, are the grandmother I know that is full of compassion and grace. If by any chance I never get to hold your hand, remember this: my love is genuine and will always stand. Get some rest now, sweet, perfect angel of mine; I will be there when Papa gathers the mule and buggy once from a sudden intertwine.

Madea was touched in a very sorrowful way. She never knew the impact that not allowing the girls to say goodbye to the Mrs. may have on them. "Come here, my darling girls. Do you know how much I love you? I will do anything if I can bring the Mrs. back. This was the time I was counting on for her to be better. The Mr. told me that only the immediate family was to see her.

The immediate family did not include my family or me. The Mr. included me as one of hers to visit her while she was dying. All the time the Mrs. took ill, there were strict rules regarding her visitors. Please forgive me if I hurt you, I wish I can mend the pieces." The girls took what Madea confessed to them and moved forward because they learned so much from the Mrs. as they matured in their ability to accept guidance.

"Gal, I understand, and we want to allow you to be hurt because of our ignorant behavior. We love you, too; that is all that matters now. You brought the Mrs. into our lives, and we are very grateful to you." Madea ate the morning meal that the girls prepared for her. She quickly bathed and dressed herself so she could sit and iron the clothes for her clients.

Madea relieved the girls from lengthy chores, although she could not do much in her last days. After all chores were completed, she went outside to enjoy the afternoon sun and the quietness of the country atmosphere. After several pregnancies, Madea knew just when the little one might come, as there would be no surprises. "I need you girls to gather all the linen from the cedar chest because the time is nearing.

Please get Johnny and Red to fetch your Papa." Little Johnny made his first trip outside of the yard with Red to find Grandpa. With his sense of smell, the hound dog and Little Johnny were quickly in tracking Grandpa. Little Johnny yelled out, "Papa, papa Gal needs you now!" Grandpa dropped his burlaps sack and pulled the contents up to a tree as he may resume later.

"A...ra good boy Johnny, make sure your sisters keep watch while I fe...fe...fetch help." Little Johnny goes back to the shack with Red at his side to tell the girls to help Gal stay calm while Grandpa fetches the midwife. Grandpa came with the help of his friend, the white fellow, and his daughter, who performed other child deliveries. "Gal, a...ra now take it easy and let Miss Marybeth do what she knows well."

The girls got all the items, as instructed by Madea, that was usable for the midwife. "Girls, you all are very good nurses. You have taken the best care of your momma; now, everybody step out while I finish." After a few moments, the baby came crying at the top of her lungs; yes, it was another girl. Grandpa was nothing but grateful and relieved to have such a strong family and a generous friend to come through for Madea and the expecting child.

Grandpa offered meat that he raised from the hog farm and a beautiful tapestry that Madea so skillfully designed. "You are an honest man, trying to raise a family with scraps and hard labor; my sincere gratitude is to you for confiding in me. Please, take those goods and feed them children. I have a special gift for you. I have a heifer. She is a milk giver. I will guide her here early tomorrow with the assistance of one of my followers."

Grandpa took great pleasure and appreciation in such a much-needed gift. He did not realize the white fellow who came to his rescue time after time was a minister. He was an angel of the lord with a compelling desire to help someone. The white fellow and his daughter gave the family their blessings and a bible that read the ministry of PWH, which is Paul Worthington Hartsfield, a minister of a local white congregation.

After reading the cover inscription, Grandpa realizes being in the company of a minister. "I a...ra knew there is something different about you sir; you helped me with my family situation so many times. We shall bless your ministry with our prayers." Madea did not say much, but there was delight in her eyes; her time with the child was exhausting.

"Thank you, sir, and Miss. When I am done resting, please let me serve you in some way." Madea and Grandpa bid the Minister and his daughter good day. Days after the youngster's birth, Madea ensured the girls continued their studies. Little Johnny, now eight years old, took to the long and tiresome walks to school with his sisters. The lessons given were very different from what they had used from the salvaged books.

Each year, the children read from a book called <u>Baby Ray</u>. The material depicts racial content as it stunts their educational goals. After weeks of attending school, Little Johnny, unlike the girls, wanted to tend to the chores rather than be bored with disgusting reading material. "Gal, I don't like that ugly tar baby on the back of this book. Why don't we have books like this from the gifts that the Mrs. gave us to read?"

Madea knew that the Negro schools were much different from the whites learning, but she wanted to instill humility into the children while they learn. "Johnny, one day you will be surrounded by scholars who have gone down the same path you once went but survived, although there may come a time when we may need your help with chores. I pray that you and your sisters get all the learning you can so you will make a choice in where you wish to work.

Little Johnny was very excited after hearing Madea build his self-worth. "I want to be a conductor like the white man in the salvaged books. He drives the train all over the countryside." Madea also knew there might be a time when the children may discontinue their schooling for a short period as their economic situation becomes bleak. "Gal, one day I will buy a big house. You and Papa will come and live there with me."

Madea was very happy to see how Johnny had grown in his desires for life, "Son, you can be anything you desire and have what you wish. Just be obedient and mine your elders." Grandpa comes home from the field earlier than usual with a grim face and disappointed outlook. Madea knew this was not the time to have unsavory news about the fieldwork as she was still nursing the baby girl.

"I a...ra got a telegram from the Mr.'s son, he will come to Georgia to make a de...de...decision about the land. Madea always and without doubt thought the best out of any situation. "When he comes, we will rest assured that what the Mrs. has given us will stand, even if the children have to stop school briefly and watch the babies while we are both working."

Madea and the oldest girls sat at the table for the late meal as Grandpa washed up. The younger girl, the dramatic one, was curious about the conversation she heard between Grandpa and Madea. "Gal, will we have to stop school and take care of the babies?" Madea just smiled, "I'm not sure right now, but I will work as much around the house with the laundry business as possible, me and Papa, so you children may get going to school.

When the time comes, we may allow the older three to take turns mining the little ones. I never want you to miss your learning. Do you really understand what I mean at this very moment? If so, come and let us sit and give thanks. Madea knew there would be rough times ahead, but she would persevere no matter how difficult the challenge might be. The next morning, after nursing the baby, Madea and the toddler gathered the antique carriage alone.

It was early April, and the air was crisp enough for a light coat and a scarf. Madea knew exactly how to dress the older children and the four-month-old baby girl; she had the experience of mothering time after time as she put the infant in the four-wheeler, and through the field, they went.

She enjoyed long walks in the park around the plantation; this was a healing process for her. Madea took advantage of the moment as she stopped to rest. She watched the older child as she ran and played in the warmth of the mid-day. Madea thought, in a gleam of whimsicality as to say, "Who am I to want everything perfect at all times, plenty of living supplies, a wonderful home, a loving husband, tolerable children, and good health?

Do I deserve this? Am I being selfish, or am I just plain scared of what is ahead? Whatever takes place at any time, I will stay calm and do what I need to do to keep my family focused on loving each other."When the sun began to warm slightly, Madea gave the oldest a sandwich, then picked the infant up from the carriage, got back seated, unbuttoned her blouse, and nursed the infant using a handy diaper for privacy.

Madea was still a young woman and had many years of bearing children. This would not be the only children in her life. As she continued to think about her life, she remembered what the Mrs. said about having more babies. "I love the thought of a big family, but I want to provide well for them all." She looked at the infant, kissed the little baby girl, and said, "Momma loves you, and I will always take care of you, my darling child."

After the child finished nursing, she softly closed her eyes and fell asleep. Madea fixed her garment and held the baby to her breast to be burped. After placing the child into the carriage, Madea and her children left the park and headed back to the shack. She was so relieved after relaxing in the coolness of the early spring with her children; she knew this was the beginning of a selfless episode in her life.

When reaching home, Madea received a hand delivery an envelope. She carefully took both children up the steps into the shack. When the older children returned home from school, there was much to accomplish as Madea spent the day enjoying the younger siblings. After supper that night, Madea told the family that she would be joining Grandpa in the fields and would be late spring.

Her decision was an effort to assist in keeping their property. She knew this might come and consciously prepared herself with no hindrances. She gave the letter to Grandpa to read to the family what she already knew. Grandpa began to read the letter as he quoted. "To the Harris family, I have decided to postpone selling all plantation houses, but make no mistake in knowing that each family who wishes to reside at the said address would by all means, take on sharecropping as payment.

I shall begin immediately with no exceptions. Thank you, W. F. Steindler jr." Little Johnny, the man in the family next to his father, spoke very courageously and said, "Gal, I would stop going to school and help Papa in the field so you can stay home and do the laundry." Madea felt as if her heart melted. She knew the children would help in any way possible.

"Thank you, my sweet little man. Your Papa and I would do just fine. Let's get ready for a good night's rest." The younger sibling was to continue breastfeeding and hand more than four months left for sucking. "Madea spoke softly to Grandpa; we may cancel school for a while because the baby needs to be cared for while we are busy in the field. She needs my breast milk and the attention of a sitter. "Gal, a...ra st...st stay with the babies until the weaning is done. We shall be...be...be fine."

Madea knew the only chance of having a secure future around the plantation was to act immediately. The next day, when she got up and made breakfast for everybody, she decided to give her last word about canceling the schooling. The children got up eager to go and work with Grandpa; they took in their morning meal, kissed Madea, and the three oldest set out with their Papa to the field.

The decision became a reality, Madea was overwhelmed; she did not expect such a warm approach to such a life-changing decision. The fieldwork went on every day throughout the end of spring and early fall until the crops were to be harvested. The baby weaned from her breast milk and made footsteps on her own. This was a step in the right direction for Madea and the family.

She thought to herself how things seem to happen overnight, "Just months prior to now, we seem to have everything: free stay here at the shack, plenty of supplies, papa with steady work, and children learning. I still have everything; I have five perfect angels and a darling husband whom I will always adore." The Mrs. was not there to give gifts or consents, but her wisdom was a legacy.

Chapter # 8

Corruption In The Worse Form

Johnny and Little Red binned together like glue. They stuck to each other from the shack to the end of the plantation and throughout the field every day; their friendship was endless. Little Johnny did not expect trouble, but after helping Grandpa and his sisters, Johnny went outside only to see Little Red all scared up, lying, panting as if chased by a predator or that of a bully.

Johnny screamed and cried because his friend was gone. Grandpa came outside and saw the horrifying sight, and touched Johnny's shoulder, and said, "Come son a...ra red is gone he won't be co...co...coming back." Johnny simply cried, "My friend, my friend, why did they hurt my friend." Grandpa knew this was a nasty prank but was in no position to do anything.

Grandpa and the rest of the family were heartbroken and wanted to know who would do such an awful thing to Red. "I a...ra will gather the digging shovel to make the grave." Johnny thought this was an opportunity to give back to red what he had always given him, as he buries his friend. "Papa, please let me bury my friend myself; this is what I need to do for him."

Grandpa gave instructions as to how the burial should be, even for an animal. After the burial, Johnny put the tools away and left the shack hurting and bitter wanting to find the perpetrators involved in hurting Red. Madea and Grandpa never thought for once that there was animal cruelty around the plantation; this was a sudden shock a real disdain. "I a...ra hope this is final and no more signs of hatred, but if it is not, I would do whatever it takes to protect my family."

Madea began to sing hymns and pray for peace and tranquility for her family. She noticed something different about the atmosphere, a sudden quietness; Johnny was not in the shack. "Papa, where is Johnny?" Grandpa grabbed the old rifle that his father gave him, a real piece of work, an antique but usable in every sense of the word. Madea and the girls were scared; she did not expect this would come to fighting.

"Do you really need your weapon; can we just go out and call for him to come home?" Johnny was determined to find the underlying cause of this nonsense to his friend Red. He had his stick as he ran, calling out to the open field, "You coward, just come and get me, you fool. Come out now." Johnny felt a hard thump just above his temple like a hard, pounding rock.

Johnny knew then there was trouble. "You did it. Why did you hurt my only friend." The intruder was a boy, a white boy about Johnny's age. "I am going to hurt you, and you best be running." When the boy pulled the sling back, Johnny ran in to the boy's midsection and began to fight vigorously with victory. When the boys were toiling and pounding, the white boy's father came out of nowhere and got Johnny off. The boy held Johnny while the boy beat him.

"You nigger shit, we will beat you just like we did that old ass hound. Now get your ass away from here." Grandpa saw Johnny staggering; his clothes all torn, his face cut, his eyes red and puffed. Grandpa did not make it in time to see what had taken place, but he swore that he would kill the baster who hurt his son if he could just find him. Grandpa began to shoot in the air, and he made three shots.

This was a signal to anyone to be aware of his retaliation for whoever came against his son. Grandpa tied the rifle around his back and took Johnny back to the shack. Madea and the girls cried and yelled, "No, they are trying to kill our family just like they did Red." Grandpa knew from experience that when he made those shots, the perpetrators would not come near his son again.

"They want to become near Johnny again. "Papa, I am not scared they were not fair. They are just cowards. Papa, I was held down so the boy would be free to fight me. They threw me to the ground, spat on me, and called me bad names." Madea was hurting intensely because of the unjust treatment from people that were potential neighbors, "Johnny, you are a brave boy, and I am very proud of you.

You have done nothing bad, but please let someone walk with you when you leave the shack." Grandpa and Madea never encouraged fights; in most cases, they insisted that the children simply avoid them. Grandpa knew Johnny was a hothead and would fight if he was tempted, but he knew the white boys were not fair most of the time.

He knew Johnny would get in fights, but he did not expect him to feel degraded or to intimidate anyone. Early the next day, Grandpa and the children left the house for another day of work. The family made sure that Johnny was in plain view throughout the day. Johnny worked the field, but he still missed his friend Red. He secretly cried and grieved for his red hound; sure enough,, red was an old dog, about sixty-three years old in dog years and nine years old in human years; he never thought red would go like that.

After the work was done, Grandpa and the children headed home. Grandpa could not get over how an adult could be so mean, whether he was white, Negro, or anybody that would willfully hold down a child so he may lose a fight. He began to cry and thought to himself, "Why did I a...ra not find them bastards putting their dirty hands on my boy?"

Madea prepared a huge feast for the working family. She thought that this was the least she could do for Johnny, his sisters, and Grandpa. When the children all settled in bed, Grandpa and Madea talked about what they would do for Johnny to replace Red. "I a...ra don't think another dog would ever replace Red unless Johnny fined it on his own."

Grandpa made a promise that he would kill the next man who put his hands on any of his children. "Gal, I would die before I let the next man hurt our son." Madea was afraid of what was going on inside of Grandpa's head; she knew he would carry out what he said if given the chance.

"Papa, surely you don't mean that; this will all pass, and you must focus on living the best life you can with your children. Johnny will be getting in more fights, and just like he came through that one, he would victoriously get through others." Grandpa looked at Madea and felt like a new man, which was all he needed: that simple talk that was long overdue.   Therapy was a help from his one and only friend his lovely wife.

"Come here, women a...ra how do you know so much; I love you, Isabella Lee Harris, you know exactly what it takes to soothe an aching heart. I fill a...ra like a rich man right now, I can a...ra accomplish any task at this very moment." Madea was so relieved she did not know how to express thanks to Grandpa.

Her eyes are all tearful, those of joy and peace, knowing that she is effectively conversing with Grandpa. "I want you to understand why we have challenges in our lives and overcome them. My darling husband, we are going to cry and hurt the rest of our lives, but understand this one thing: we are strong, we endure, we teach, and we give of ourselves because of self-sacrifice.

This type of strange and unforeseen situation will come again; we will be ready spiritually and physically. There has never a time when hardship, sickness, or discontentment has played a part in our lives that we have not gone through without each other and coming out victoriously.

I will always be here for you and the children until that beckoning moment; my love will endure endlessly. Johnny has everything any child could possess, and that is the love of both of us, so please let's just enjoy our family and make the most of what we have." Grandpa saw the urgency in Madea's eyes and knew that honesty and contentment was a virtue that she possessed, "Gal a...ra I want to give back to you what you have given me these years; with so little, you have taught me how to fight within myself and win.

You a...ra are precious to me, I will get through the hatred that I have built up; I will find a way to let go now." Madea and Grandpa gently held and caressed each other immensely. They entrusted themselves in a relationship that builds on love and character, the kind that they are trying to instill in their children. Madea had reservations about having more children in the past because of the economic structure of their life.

After the conversation with Mrs. Steindler, she knew that with all the love and affection they had between each other they would manage somehow to feed, clothe, and give each one of their children expanded love. They will have the necessities even if it took all she had to fight and keep fighting. "Honey, I knew we would have more children, even a large family; now I pray for health and stability in their lives.

When you brought Johnny home, all beaten up, my heart ached, but the family that caused this infliction has something worse to overcome. We have a precious jewel in our family, an exotic stone. We don't have to start a battle, only end one because our children has value a jewel of self-advancement because of what you and I have taught them. I never thought that I would have to say this; I really feel sorry for the boy who fought Johnny with the help of his father.

I believe he feels cheated just like Johnny felt when you brought him home. This kind of feeling is nothing but hatred because he feels he cannot fight because his daddy will always cheat for him the rest of his natural life. Our children will never start a fight and will never need assistance from either of us to help defend them. I pray that this fool of a parent that teaches this child hatred would come to a point in his life that he is plainly scared and is afraid to let his son see that color is not the enemy."

Madea smiled and began to do some late chores; she prepared the night pot for a fresh clean as she cleaned the "slop jar" with fresh potash soap and lavender fragrance, leaving sufficient well water in the bottom of the pot for the family's use. With many unique ideas and desires to change his family's lifestyle, Grandpa thought he would one day provide a common way of meeting personal needs.

He wanted to use running water in his house as a toilet to sit and flush, just like the Steindlers when he visited them during the family's loss. As Grandpa often stuttered when conversing, Madea, with her wonderful wit and wisdom, helped to improve and minimize his habit of stuttering.

"I will a...ra take what I have to build a proper toilet for my family with my hands, I a...ra will bring running water, a spigot into my house." Madea was impressed as she listened to Grandpa's ambitious futuristic abilities, but most of all, she was amazed at how well his speech was except for a...ra in his conversation; otherwise, it was almost perfect. After taking in for the night, Grandpa and Madea made way for the bed as he blew out the kerosene lamp.

The morning light was just hours away Grandpa and the children had fieldwork to do. Madea tended the house affairs and the younger siblings. Madea awakened as she normally did, prepared breakfast, and started her day's chores.

Johnny was very outgoing; he knew exactly what to do when he had his fill of breakfast. Johnny ran out drew the water from the well, and made his rounds as he fed the chickens.

Grandpa knew he could depend on Johnny. He did not have much to offer his children in preparing them in furthering their education, but he gave them the necessary tools to care for themselves by teaching them how to work for their needs as field hands and other areas of the plantation.

Johnny was only ten years old when education was needed, but the family was at a time when there were only the bare necessities of life, including only food supplies. The children had to drop school to help their parents maintain and survive because a period when rationing food was at its worst.

Grandpa was the only adult working as Madea was with child again in her sixth pregnancy. The oldest siblings assisted Madea and helped with the laundry and whatever Madea was able to bring in from reliable patrons. Grandpa insisted that Johnny would continue working in the field next to him because he was the male child and big for his age.

"Johnny, a...ra I want you to be my right-hand man, can you handle that?" Johnny honored Grandpa and thought he was the center of his life next to Madea. "Papa, I am ready. I want to help you work the field; just tell me what to do." Madea wanted Johnny to learn how to be responsible, but she knew he was very young and innocent when there were major problems.

He had a lot to learn, and it took more than a day in the field with his father. "Wait just one minuet, young man; you will not stray too far away from your papa, and please listen well to whatever instructions he may have for you." Johnny appreciated the lectures, but Grandpa talked very candidly with him after dealing with the bad fight he encountered. Johnny answered Madea as if he did not know what to expect the first time.

"Yes mam, I want stray away from Papa." The next day, Grandpa and Johnny worked well in the field. Johnny was so excited about pleasing Grandpa that he did everything just to hear him say well done, my son. Johnny worked every day close to Grandpa just as if Madea asked him to do.

It was a time when there was nothing of value to spare. Food was a priceless commodity and the tenants had to work even harder to remain in their spaces and provide for their families. Even the harvest had fallen short; families had to do without precious items such as medical supplies when everything had a ration sticker.

The drayman would risk his job and freedom as he dumped needful items under the houses of tenants that he knew, as this was a help in securing food for the poor families. Madea took the scraps, prepared quick meals, and preserved as much as possible to accommodate her family's other meals.

She often reminds her family not to waste even a single crumb but to preserve it whenever appropriate. Wages was not issued in money because the property was the ownership of the Steindler's and working the field was a way of paying for their stay as tenants. They supplied much food for only those who resided on the plantation. Johnny and Grandpa took scraps for the hogs when this was the only source to feed them.

Johnny and Grandpa did not expect trouble in the field, especially when there was hunger. It was so apparent not only to poor Negroes, but this monstrosity of an event plagued the whites and also limited the rich and well-to-do. At the end of the day, Johnny and Grandpa took their croaker sacks filled with food and scraps and headed home.

Grandpa did not know that he would have to fight; moreso, this happened around his son. The two men, both White bullies, stopped Grandpa and Johnny and said, "You best be putting them dam croaker bags down and handing them over, you hungry ass bastards." Grandpa was at a test at this point; he always taught Johnny to avoid fights and scuffles and simply walk away.

He wanted the thieves to leave when he spoke because he knew Johnny would never back down even if he had to fight. "You a...ra leave now, I a...ra don't want no trouble, and we want be giving up our goods. Johnny, a...ra take these sacks." When the two bullies struck Johnny with his bat across his leg, Grandpa grabbed the one bully, snatched the bat picked him up threw him to the ground and held him in a chokehold.

"If you a...ra touch that boy I will kill this nasty son-of-a-bitch." The assailants knew Negroes were afraid to kill whites for fear of hatred and unjust opportunities. "My papa said leave now." Johnny was a hot head, fast and ready to defend what was his "Give me that sack, you dam nigger or I will beat the shit out of you."

Johnny knew what it took to bring the coward down. "I said leave me and my Papa right now." After one punch in his groin, Johnny's opponent got the message; when the pain felt unbearable, the coward staggered away and physically bruised with strong discomfort. Grandpa could have killed the bully if he held him any longer.

When he eased off his assailant, the bully got up and ran. Grandpa grew concerned about Johnny's leg after watching the intruder strike him with the bat. "Can you walk son?"

The bullies hit Johnny just below the kneecap, bruising only the less delicate area. "I can walk Papa. He did not stop me from defending what was mine." Grandpa put the croaker sacks on his back and went off as if nothing happened.

He knew this type of meanness would persist because the shortage of food and supplies was prevalent even in the well-to-do families. The Steindler' was wealthy, but they had to endure the economical blitz of rationing supplies as well as the common people. "Papa I want our lives to be as they were last year, do you, and why can't we get paid for our labor."

Grandpa appreciated that Johnny asked a question that he should have known early on. It was not Grandpa and Madea's intent to keep their children in suspense regarding the rationing period; they simply wanted their family to understand that no matter how life circumstances may appear, a sense of responsibility must take place among even those less fortunate.

"Johnny a...ra when you were a tot, your first spanking was because you didn't obey Gal and me. Now, you had a responsibility, even as a two-year-older, to do what was right to do no matter how the grass looked over on the other side. You could have taken to a dangerous fate even as a wee one. We loved you then and love you today because we are responsible parents. Gal and I have to accept what the law says about cutting back on food and supplies, which means rationing for all families, rich and poor.

I will explain more when we reach the shack so the girls can get equal understanding." When Grandpa and Johnny arrived, Madea thought Johnny had gotten into a serious fight again. "Papa, what brings this kind of situation? Did you not obey your papa and remain by his side? What's going on, what's wrong?" Grandpa was not interested in answering any question; his focus was to get help for Johnny's wounds, he did not know the extent of the bruise on his leg. "Gal, a...ra please not now we need help for Johnny's leg.

He has a very nasty wound. I will tell you what happened later." Madea and the girls gathered clean clothes and some of her special liniments that she made for burns and cuts and bad sores. Madea washed the wound and applied the homemade ointment and bandages so the leg would not infect. Grandpa made a pair of makeshift crutches for Johnny to use while his injuries subsided.

Grandpa did not want to alarm Madea and the girls, but he gathered the family around the supper table and told Madea exactly what had happened regarding the two bullies. He explained how they tried to intimidate a young boy and his father by using blunt force, and harsh language and how Johnny took charge and helped him out of a crisis. He told the family how proud he was of Johnny.

"Johnny a...ra helped save our goods from two thieves; he did not give in. I would be doomed a...ra without Johnny at my side. Madea thought this was a terrible risk for both Johnny and Grandpa. "This is not good; when I have the baby, we must let the children start their studies again. I am sure the law would be different at that time. Food rationing would cease, and the younger children could tag along with us."

Grandpa was not as optimistic as Madea; he knew how the system operated, and it has not been determined how long food rationing would be. Gal, a...ra the children need to know about our living arrangements with the Steindlers and how it will be affecting us during the rationing period."

Grandpa and Madea did not purposely deny the children from knowing why there was no wages for their hard work but insisted that they learn how to tolerate sudden changes in their lives. "Before Papa and I left our home that we thought was his inheritance, little did we know or understand that the property belonged to the state.

However, with the help of his friend, we came to understand and tolerate why sudden obstacles arose in our lives. We could have very well lived in the space for the rest of our lives if there were written documents.

Papa and I did not know how to communicate and read then, but thanks to the missionaries at the church and their time and concern, they gave me hope. I self-taught myself by searching and raiding the dump pile looking for readable material. The oldest girl was so impressed with how far her parents had come in their quest to make reading available for her and her siblings that she began to cry with amazement.

"Papa, I am sorry that you had to prove your worth to those bullies, but I believe no matter how bad a fight you took on, you would never let anyone ever again take away what is yours. Gal, I am proud of you and Papa for sharing such a wonderful experience with us. I love you."

Chapter # 9

The Enticement

It was a day of uncertainty when Grandpa got up to start out for work; he knew Madea would need his help because of the untimely chance of giving birth while he was in the field. Johnny's wounds were all well, and there was no sign of malfunction in his movement. Nevertheless, Grandpa insisted that Johnny remain home with Madea and the girls until he felt sure that there were no setbacks while working all day in the field. It was a dark and windy day, but Grandpa had to keep going because there was another mouth to feed, another bundle of joy added to the family.

The girls were Madea's right hand now that she was ready to deliver. Medea woke up and saw how the children took on themselves without request and done all the chores while she rest. The second oldest girl the dramatic one, made flapjacks for Madea and milk from the cow as she learned to jug the heifer while watching Madea and Grandpa. "I must have lain back down after Papa took to the field.

Thank you, my lovely children, for looking out for me and making my breakfast. Madea had no idea that she would deliver today; after she finished her breakfast, she had an extreme urge to relieve herself. When she stepped to the floor, she felt the water break, the same with all her pregnancies. "Johnny, how is your leg; can you walk to the field?

I need your Papa; please hurry!" The girls knew what to do from past deliveries, as they helped comfort Madea while waiting for Grandpa and the midwife. "Gal, I remember how the midwife felt your belly before the baby came. Can we assist you in the delivery this time?" Madea was unsure what to do; she was slightly in pain.

Finding a midwife would be difficult during food rationing, even if there are prior arrangements.

When Johnny reached Grandpa, he called out to him with urgency as he did with the last child. When Grandpa heard Johnny, he knew it was Madea ready to deliver. "Johnny a...ra is Gal ready for the midwife?" Johnny did not know how far along Madea was with contractions, but he knew he had to bring back Grandpa.

Johnny grabbed Grandpa's croaker bag and said, "Papa, I can work the field while you fetch the midwife, please Papa, let me." Grandpa had no choice; in fact, he was delighted to know that Johnny was able to take over. "Now Johnny a...ra just remember what we talked about."

Johnny was happy to get out of the house, even if it was a minuet; he had to prove to his papa that he could do it alone. "Yes sir, I won't forget, I will be careful." Grandpa left things in Johnny's hands while fetching Madea a midwife. Grandpa warned Johnny about the persistence of undue turmoil resulting from the rationing period. Johnny finished his chores in the field and had time to play so he thought.

While hanging with his friends he never thought for a moment what an impact it would have on the family if he got in a deathly fight. After seeing the pink in the skies, he realized his papa would come looking and asking questions. "I got to leave right now. I won't disappoint my Papa." Johnny grabbed the croaker sacks and ran back to the shack like a rabbit. Just as Johnny entered the door, Grandpa had already grabbed his cap and jacket.

Grandpa was stern when provoked; he knew other young boys were hanging around the work site, but he simply asked a question. "Johnny, did you finish your chores and hang out with the other fellows?" Johnny wanted to deny the truth, but he remembered what Madea always said about being honest.

"Yes Papa, I played with some boys I met while I was finishing the field work." Grandpa began to stutter a little. "A...ra did I not say to you keep to yourself, finish the chore, and come home? You should have come home a...ra two hours ago. Do you remember what Gal and I always say to you about hardheadiness? A...ra yes, a hard head makes a soft ass.

You a...ra will be working again in the field without me." Johnny knew what this meant.

He disobeyed Grandpa through the years, and the chastisement was awful but a lesson to be learned. Johnny saw his new sibling, a girl; he began to realize how much Grandpa would need him to keep the chores going. Madea was all tired out from the birthing and the girls, tending to the cleaning, and putting away the dishes from supper.

This moment reminds Johnny just how selfish he was and how he could lose all of it by putting himself in harm's way if Grandpa withheld the importance of his character.

Grandpa insisted that Johnny wash up, grab a plate, and eat his supper. "The girls a...ra made a hardy meal for the family so sat and ate." After Johnny finishes eating, he has a sense of urgency that haunts him inside.

He dedicated his effort to extra chores to make up for his disobedience.

"Papa, I like to jug the cow and refresh her grazing trough before settling for bed tonight. I will give the slop jar fresh clean for Gal and the girls." Grandpa saw Johnny's desire to make up for the irresponsibility he acquired in the field so he simply said, "Go a...ra to bed, son; tomorrow is soon enough." The next morning, Johnny moved before Grandpa and Madea, even the new baby so as not to disturb the family. He went about the chores as he cut wood for the wood-burning stove and brought in logs for the fireplaces.

Grandpa knew Johnny was very eager to help with the outside chores, but it is a triumph to instill the appreciation of care from his parents into a young boy. Johnny's only association with other children his age was those around the field. After tending the chores, Johnny returned to the shack for breakfast only to have Madea converse with him.

"Come here, Johnny. I haven't seen you since last evening. Did you get to meet your new sister? I rested during your talk with Papa, but I heard things we can discuss. Would that be okay with you?" Johnny loves both Grandpa and Madea very dearly and with great respect. He had a zest when Madea spoke to him because she had a great reception in her purpose.

Madea knew that Johnny desired to experience life even as he worked in the field. "My darling son, there are so many undesirable trials we must face in this life, but the truth is that although you may come in contact with friends and associates, my advice is to be very careful.

No one out of these four walls will ever love you like Papa and I". Johnny had great patience and captured more with just one sentence from Madea's short little speech than he would ever receive from Grandpa. He knew Grandpa meant well, but after years of being around Madea and not having his papa during segments in his life as a toddler, he presented a great impact on a young boy in the early growing years of his life.

"I know that you will face challenges as you step out in the world, but know and understand that Papa will always be there in spirit and love, and so will I." After Johnny and Madea's conversation comes to an end, the new baby screams for her attention. The girls took charge and made their way to Madea's beside to receive the infant as she prepared herself to nurse the baby.

"Thank you, Gal, I will do what you ask of me. I will never let you down. I love you and Papa, too." Johnny made it possible for the girls to start the morning meal by kindling a fire in the wood-burning stove. They learn just as Madea taught them how to prepare breakfast and tend their new sibling.

Grandpa admired all his children at that moment and presented a vow to each of them. "I have a mean streak in me a...ra regarding my children, but I want each of you to be happy and safe. A...ra there is temptation out there, and it is not so kind.

I will never let any harm come to either of you if I had to die trying to prove my point." Madea took the child after nursing her, gave the infant that motherly pamper, and placed her in the wooden cradle that Grandpa built as a family heirloom. After breakfast, Johnny and the other siblings gathered around to hear some interesting news about returning to school.

Madea and Grandpa tell the family their plans to continue to meet the needs of the workloads. "Johnny, do you remember the dreams you had when the angel bid you her blessings? Don't worry, and you will be fine?" It had been years since Johnny had such dreams, and there was no knowledge of angels appearing in his last dream.

"Gal, I can only say maybe because I don't remember." Madea simply laughed and said, "Well, I had quite a conversation with an angel just after the baby arrived; she gave me the same blessings that she gave you." The girls were so excited they wanted to hear more. "She said not to worry and this would be a prosperous year for all of us.

Papa and I agree to send you back to school very soon. I believe the government will lift the ration period, and things will be normal again." Johnny did not take well to the news, but he did not want to discourage the rest of the family. He simply had other plans for his time. Madea notices a quite grim look, not so accepting, on Johnny's face, but she continues to focus on her plans for the children.

"I want each of you to continue in your studies, and Papa and I will make our way together back to the field." The children sang songs, danced, and simply took what Madea said and moved forward, especially the dramatic one, the second oldest one. "I am going to teach school, sing, and dance just like you, Gal."

Madea kept her eye on Johnny as to say I know what your thinking is. When all the excitement comes to an end, Madea calls Johnny to her side, "Johnny, your Papa and I have worked the field before you and your sisters were conceived, and one day, there won't be a field for any of us to work.

I know how you love Papa and me and desire to help, but it is okay to let go. Papa and I will do just fine; you have proved to us the male you are time after time. I would like you and the girls to focus on your studies as you are behind at present. Now, there may come a time when an emergency may arise. Then we may call on your expertise, so give yourself a break and let the grownups take care of you for a while."

Johnny seems very accepting of his and Madea's private conversation. He receives all the comforting attributes about himself that Madea delivers very well. He began to cry, "Gal, all I wanted to do is help you because I want you to rest and stay at the house. I love you and Papa and I know you tire sometimes, but I thank you for helping me see this differently."

Grandpa and the girls went about their normal business as not to notice Madea and Johnny's little talk. Grandpa and Madea want to give Johnny something for his extra effort in helping the family get back on their feet. "Johnny, a...ra, we won't be attending the field today; it is time we get a...ra some chores done for the coming summer."

Johnny notices the girls' silly little giggles and excitement while making their beds. Madea does not care for animals in the house, but she tolerates the surprise Grandpa and the girls' store for Johnny. Grandpa played a little trick on Johnny, saying, "Johnny a...ra grab that chain and let us go outside." When Johnny began to pull the chain, he felt quite a resistance coming from the opposite end.

There is a puppy when Johnny puts more force on his end of the chain. "Gal, papa, a little puppy, is this mine." Johnny was so happy; he noticed the sex of the animal and wanted to name him immediately. "Thank you, Papa. I am going to name him Bob because he has a short bobtail." After Johnny gets the puppy going, he realizes why the girls laugh so much. He had so much spirit after the talk with Madea and after receiving the special surprise.

The little dog needs a home, and Johnny needs something to care for and call his own. "I know this gift will never replace Little Red, but he can keep Johnny busy and give him something more meaningful to look forward to." Grandpa agrees and feels the experience in the field was a lesson for Johnny as it contributes to trouble as a "disorder." Johnny loves the outside, especially when tending to his new friend; he watches his pet carefully.

"I will never let anybody take you away, you little bobtail rascal. Gal, please, may I sleep with my pup outside in the pen tonight? He is mine, and I do not want anything to come of him."Just like the average mother, Madea disapproves of her child in the night, all alone with a new puppy. "Johnny! Bob is a dog, and pets will always possess that outside nature. An animal enjoys a habitat you and I can only observe and never compete.

He can dig and relieve himself without worrying about cleaning up; therefore, the elements of the outdoors can be a bit challenging for a boy who has never gone camping or lives under unstable conditions. I do not mean this area is bombarded by constant humility, but it could be enticement if you are alone outside. Before Madea could finish her thought, Johnny intercedes.

"I want to leave the shack. I will stay put."Papa and I cannot put you and your sisters in harm's way knowing how the bullies humiliated you when your leg received bruises only weeks ago." Johnny reminded Madea of her dream when the angel said things would be better; she should not worry.

"I am glad to know that you pay attention to our conversation, but my answers are purely based on what Papa and I have talked about daily." Grandpa and Madea knew how attached to the new puppy Johnny might concentrate on schoolwork and less on taking on adult responsibilities.

"Johnny, a...ra, this is a good time to get Bob in his new home by moving the kennel next to the house out of the sight of predators while you are away at school. You will a...ra have your moment to train him after your studies and chores. Remember, you will a...ra have plenty of time to do fieldwork when it is necessary."

Johnny knew his parents desired the best for him and his siblings. Therefore, accepting such a milestone in his life is appreciative when Madea and Grandpa exhibit value and love. His dream of becoming a conductor surfaces and motivates a desire to follow it. Johnny had no idea how Madea and Grandpa planned to work the field and mind the little ones, but he trusted their wisdom and guidance by not questioning their judgments.

Madea looks at Grandpa with amazement; she knows the conversation she and Grandpa instilled in Johnny was effective. They saw how his growth in maturity and self-reliance characterized him as a son and the person they raised. After Johnny left their presence to tend to the puppy, Madea took Grandpa's hand and and said, "I am so thankful to you and how you stand by our children, especially Johnny. He has come a long way because of what he sees in us as parents.

As I declared before, Johnny will face unforeseen obstacles in his life, but they are a part of his growth. He knows the difference between the wrong and right by observing our lives. I am going to take every chance I have to display positive influences around my family." Grandpa hugs Madea, kisses her forehead, and admits his prior mistakes when he was unfaithful and how she helps him overcome them all.

"Gal, a...ra your compassion and strength a...ra overwhelms me, my unfaithfulness you forgave because you believes in me. I see why our son is so dedicated in accepting our plan to care for him and his sisters because of your unwavering faith." The older girls take turns in assisting Madea with the new baby and the two younger children.

The girls observe her care at previous moments when this might be a useful tool one day. They also seem unsure of how Madea and

Grandpa could maintain sharecropping without their help caring for the little ones. Madea nurses the infant and welcomes the help from the girls, but she insists the school prioritizes their lives. "Gal, who will you get to mind the baby while you have to work the field?

If we are in school, nobody won't be around to nurture the little ones and watch out for them. I can mind them as I read to them while you and Papa work the field; please give me a chance to show how I can be a relief for the family."

Madea knew how the children wished to help maintain a simple lifestyle and have fewer worries about rationing supplies. "My sweet child, I want to give my three oldest a start in life; you, your brother, and sister will not miss any more time from school, which is a promise. I pray that we will soon get through this ordeal so there will be no more talk about missing school."

Madea remembered the day Johnny and Grandpa returned after the thieves wrestled them for their goods. She did not want this type of surprise to affect the girls and take their innocence from them. "Your papa and I have a plan to feed this family and keep with our responsibilities to maintain our stay on the plantation. I will tell you a story about a very young mother and her little baby and how she survives on values."

Madea knew when she offered to tell a story of any sort. The children were all ears, attentive, and acquirable. "When I met your papa, I brought with me a little girl, about six months old and quite pale. Your papa welcomes my child into his life just as he did me because there is unconditional love between us. We built our lives on values, but more than that, we built those things that are intrinsic.

What is more important to us as a couple? When I went to work in the field, my whole family took center stage because my heart was genuinely desiring to help in any way possible. I knew Papa loved me and provided very well, so I made the load less tedious for him as I suck the baby, bundled her right in the field, and continued my daily chores.

I try to work as though our needs may soon falter; just like you, I wish I could carry on in the field by helping him. I take on great responsibilities as a helper but not much of a mother and wife. Things that are intrinsic and valuable are those of love and admonishment.

This is a time to receive as much from your studies as possible, dream, and create your values. Please, I urge each of you to look forward to enjoying your time learning. Dismiss the lure from your lives, and dream big.

Chapter # 10

A Mothers Dream

It is a September morning, Madea and Grandpa prepare the oldest children for their day back on the road to continue their education. There is no forethought of the economy; the depression period persists, but having the children in pursuit of their future is all Madea' dreams. She knew that without the help of the children it would be hard to maintain the workload with two toddlers and a nursing baby.

Madea remembers how she made doable the appetite to succeed when their family depends on just her unsinkable wit. She takes her babies as once before and bundles them, and uses her petite body as a sleigh while she performs her work. This method is a legacy that she uses while she observes her ancestors. Grandpa saw how serious Madea's plan was to keep things going as a helpmate and a loving wife; he also administered caution and integrity because there was still hunger and diversity in their mist.

"Gal, a...ra we may have some trouble from thieves desiring our goods, but I will protect you and the babies. I will take the toddlers and provide a bed for them to rest while I pull them as we gather the crop." Once again, Madea welcomes Grandpa's idea; she knows there are ways to get through problematic situations if they both come to an agreeable solution. "Good, that works fine;

I can carry the baby under my breast in a sling as I have during previous field chores." Madea and Grandpa took charge daily during the food shortages as they implemented ways to continue their lives and teach their children the value of hard work and education. As ironic as it seems, there is always some type of fieldwork around the plantation, even during a period of distress as the property owner catches a setback in supplies.

"I suspect a...ra this season, old man Steindler's son may change his mind about us living on the plantation and allow paying people to reside in our stead. There is a shortage of supplies even for the rich man to maintain his employee security during this ration period." Madea knew Grandpa's insinuations may purely be from denial, and not realizing this too shall pass.

Grandpa is hurt inside as he observes his family, even the newborn, out in the environmental elements as he and Madea makeshift themselves as a babysitter as they work. She also knew that Grandpa honors her desires and dreams for the children's education, even if it means making an impossible situation possible. She softly spoke to Grandpa as she prepared for a quick meal while removing the sling that held the baby under her small frame.

"Papa, let's rest a minute and feed the babies. I will give the toddlers a bite to eat and suck the baby; there is plenty of fixing in the can for our snacks too." Grandpa releases the sling that binds his waist as he pulls the toddlers during his working chore. When Madea finishes nursing the child and pampers her, she makes her way to feed the rest of the family after refreshing herself with prepared water from the packed meal.

"Honey, I am proud of you for giving the children a chance to get out to further their learning by attending the schoolhouse. I know how it bothers you inside to see your babies in the midst of the elements just to keep my dream alive when you and Johnny can very well take on the total workload. We both know that Johnny has to learn even if the girls take to the road alone." Grandpa began to intervene abruptly and simply said, "Gal, a...ra do you think I will send the girls alone without the support of their brother in this time of uncertainty? I want the same for all of the children, and I will think of a way to change our operation as we do with what we have now." Grandpa knew when he spoke of the Steindler's integrity regarding their reneging on a promise to continue housing his family as they reside on the property; however, Madea would have a say in the matter as well.

"Gal, a...ra I am sorry for speaking out of such a rage about the Steindlers. Madea lays the baby on the soft cushioning matt and walks towards Grandpa while the girls play in their presence. She passionately caresses him and says, "It is okay to release what's ever on your mind, and we can discuss things if we feel broken in spirit. Let us never hold them inside or feel discouraged about life's challenges."

Grandpa felt as if he owed Madea an explanation of the way he commented on the Steindler's character. I a...ra am thankful for the decency of their family, and I hope their experience during the depression will not be a drastic hold on their business." Grandpa and Madea took the children, placed them into their original harness, and returned to continue the workloads.

After finishing the chores, Madea and Grandpa made their way home carrying the children as they were deep in sleep. Johnny and the girls will not reach the plantation until the sun hides over the clouds because of such a long walk. Madea took rations that the drayman purposely dumped under the elevated house as a gift to poor families. She sorts those useful items, prepares supper for her family, and distributes scrapes for the animals.

She milks the heifer and bottles the milk for the family's breakfast with Grandpa assisting. Madea and Grandpa's desire to build their family and give them the necessities presents a huge problem. There is no money, and supplies are scarce. Madea never looked back on past imperfections. She simply took all she had and went forth as if nothing was out of the norm.

"I will set this table and give the best that I can to my family with what is provided. We will eat, get full, and I will gather the scraps that remain for our next meal." Madea took flour sacks that she had previously preserved and made dresses for herself and the girls. She was skillful with her hands, but she and Grandpa possessed little educational skills to tend employment besides field hands.

"My dream is to see that all my children learn to fend for themselves and their offspring on what Papa and I have given them. We will carry on and push them without thinking of dropping their goals and ambitions." On days the school closes, the children contribute their energy to helping Grandpa collect manure to fertilize their space on the plantation.

The space provides a garden that supplies fresh produce as it helps feed and nourish the entire family. The children continue to outgrow their clothes and rely on what Madea is able to gather and patch. There is no money until slaughtering season, and Grandpa markets his hogs. The children each receive a winter coat and a pair of boots as they attend school and church.

Grandpa, as he stutters, is so proud to provide the least thing for his children, "I a...ra can take this meat and make a sell to keep the children warm and fill their stomachs on what we raise from the land." This is the only monetary gift, only by selling the family's food as Grandpa and Madea scrapes to feed the animals. Madea knew the meat had its boundaries, which meant families could only purchase if, by chance, there is a well-to-do source or a group wanting to share in their efforts to divide their earnings.

"Papa, we are fortunate to have the meat from our hogs at this time, but we have enough meat to hand to someone to render some of our blessings. We want to be able to sell all of what is needed to purchase necessities, but I am thankful for what is provided." Grandpa had to work the field and give his share to the Steindlers for giving the family space on the plantation.

He could not sell enough of the meat to make huge purchases or pay the Steindlers for allowing the family to live on the property, but he had the support from Madea as she reminds him; "Papa, it is not always how much you have, but what you do with what is given to you." Madea often refers to Grandpa as Papa around the children, especially the toddlers, so their tender ears may adapt to hearing as she repeats his position in the house.

When Grandpa and Johnny gather the scraps from a slaughter, Bob gets his prize for being a helpful friend and pet. Johnny has little time to spend with his friend because of what happens to Red, his first pet. "Papa, I will bring the babies out so they may help Johnny feed Bob and get to know him as a loving pet." Madea gave the two toddlers and the nursing infant a tour around the space where the animals may get a smell of their presence.

She claims that an animal will hurt a child for fear of dominance if he cannot recognize them as family members or friends. This means that the family has to be cautious while allowing the toddlers to get to know the family's pet. Grandpa and Madea believe an animal will be your protector if given a chance to eat from your hand or lick your sores when there are cuts or leg lesions.

Madea assures the dog while being extra careful feeding him. "Quiet Bob, they are your family too, good boy, just be calm. We just want to feed you." After Bob ate from the toddler's hands, they were able to pet him and rub his coat as he licked their faces. "Well done, see how well that was. He just wants to love; okay now, let's go inside and clean up." After she allows the children to feed the dog, she insists they come with her as she takes hold of them with her free hand while holding the nursing baby.

"No Gal, I want to feed Bob some meat; let go." The dog obviously thought Madea was trying to mistreat the children as she requested that they come inside the shack and clean up. He barks profusely at Madea. "Johnny, come now, I am not able to stop the agitation. He wants to fight; please quiet him."Grandpa and Johnny came out running like they were about to extinguish a fire.

Johnny spoke quietly and said, "Good boy, okay, they are your friends too." Grandpa sees how Madea pulls the toddlers and says, "Gal, a...ra let go, leave the little ones and walk away." The dog began to calm down immediately, stopped barking, and lay on his back, kicking and rolling. Madea realizes what is happening; she simply says, "Come, children, we will feed Bob again tomorrow, okay."

The children were agreeable, and so was the dog. Grandpa took the leash and collar that was prepared for Red and placed them on Bob. He began to talk quietly to himself, "I a...ra believe this is a good hand me down even for you; everybody needs something already used." Bob smells the scent he detects from the previous owner and accepts the hand-me-down without reservations.

After all the excitement, Madea prepares for a moment of serenity as the oldest girl sets the table for a family picnic. This is a time to relax even though there was a brief calamity with the pet dog. "I know that Bob will never harm the children or me, I simply caught him off guard. I see the true love and protection this animal gives to our loved ones. We will enjoy this picnic and give thanks for what we have and what we desire most in this life."

Bob began another episode of uneasy and raging sparks of agitation; he had never acted so unpleasant and fearful. Grandpa knew there must be something from an animal's perspective that Bob sensed as an animal, which he could not at that very moment. When Grandpa went for his rifle, there was a figure in the distance and that of a person. Grandpa bid Bob to remain at rest.

"A...ra stay put, Bob, and let us sees what comes this way, stay now." When the figure gets visible, it cries out for assistance, a white man all torn and appears to have an unpleasant situation. "Help me, please. Can you help me now!" Bob begins to bark again but in a compromising way when Grandpa simply says, "Calm down, boy, sit and be good." Grandpa calls for Johnny as he and Grandpa were props for the man to rest on as he walks toward the rest of the way.

"Thank you; may I have some water and food?" Madea saw the devastation of dealing with the man and, without hesitation, came to his rescue with vital needs. Madea insists on giving to the needs of her neighbors as she contends that this giving will come back to them someday. "Grandpa and Johnny gently prop the man to the picnic bench while Madea offers cool well water and fixings from their family meal.

Johnny seems very inquisitive and wants to know what happen and why this individual chose their home for help. "What happened to you, sir; did someone mug you and take your goods? Why did you come in this direction? Why, sir, did you not holler for help? Somebody could have the help that you need much sooner. As wise as she is, Madea thought Johnny must give this man a moment to get his strength and that he would talk as soon as their help satisfied him.

"Johnny, he must eat and drink. I believe in time, he will tell us about the ordeal that caused him to be in this condition. "Mam, I am much obliged for your hospitality, but there is trouble brewing near this plantation. Be aware for the sake of your boy children. I heard a dog barking about an hour ago while I lay unconscious, and then I knew there was someone nearby who may lend me a helping hand.

I followed the sound of the dog until it stopped, but I continued on this path, hoping that somebody would spot me and assist me. I came to a nasty halt when my car tire blew out just miles away. I fell and lay unconscious after hitting my head against the dash. I was very lucky to crawl from under the car. Grandpa relates to the man when he found Johnny all tattered and beaten up with no one in sight and simply waiting for help.

He remembers the devastation he felt just knowing that there could be someone so vicious to leave a boy without help just left to perish. "Mr., what a...ra is your business in these parts, if you know of such shortcomings about boy children? Madea thought the family owed the man at least a bit of rest for the information, "Papa, let us give him a chance to lay his head on the table to rest, and he may be able to tell us more after he sleeps."

After clearing the table, Madea notices the color come back in the man's face; immediately, his eyes open. Madea thought someone might start to wonder where he was and acquire information about him. Madea spoke softly as she seemingly was concerned about his well-being, "Mr. I can truly tell you that our family does not own any form of transportation, but if you desire to mat here on the table, I will bring you a quilt and pillow with a blanket. My husband will borrow the neighbor's mule and buggy to get you to the sheriff so you may receive further help and medical attention."

Madea was curious about what the man states to her and Papa when he appeared earlier. Mr. I need to know more about what you say about our child's safety; Johnny is my only son. Please tell me if you know something that will keep him out of harm's way. "Mam, all I can say is to make sure he is with other family members while he is out roaming.

I believe he would be fine if he were around those who love him rather than isolated. He will be much safer among numbers. Madea did not dismiss her concerns but she knew the girls would keep her and Grandpa informed if there are unsavory business near their route to and from the schoolhouse. "Mr., what did you see that alarms you at this time, and why did you not report it to the sheriff?"

The man got a bit nervous and less informative, "Mam, I did not see much, but please take my advice as I have already spoken, and your family will be fine. Madea knew that Johnny had a dirty encounter with a father and son several years ago, but Grandpa swore that no one would come near Johnny again because of his gunshot threats. Madea knew it might be a different issue, according to what the man previously stated.

Mam, if it pleases you, I will give this information to the authorities, and that is all the help I have for your family. Grandpa and Johnny come out to find out more about the man and to see if Madea recovers more information from the man regarding trouble that may consume boys. "Mr., we know nothing of such brewings around here, but if you can render the same service to our neighbors as we bestow to you in your time of need by carrying out your word to inform the sheriff, then our boy and others can live in harmony."

While the man continues to rest, Grandpa and Johnny leave the shack to borrow the neighbor's buggy. Just as they took to the road, the dog started a snarl and began to bark uncontrollably as though intruders were approaching. Madea knew there might be something to alarm the dog so abruptly; she hoped Grandpa would bring back some news revealing why Bob continued to fuss. "Quiet Bob, Papa, and Johnny will be back soon; just calm down now."

Grandpa and Johnny come back home as they sit in the rear seats of the sheriff's car while he escorts them to the shack. When the sheriff enters the yard, he demands that Grandpa and Johnny remain seated until he uncovers the mystery behind the accident with no occupant inside. "Good day sir; I see you have my husband and son. What is the problem."

The sheriff was crude and had little respect for the family, "These boys claim they know where the driver of the accident that happens up the road there." Bob continues to bark as to tear down the fence while the sheriff questions Madea. "Shut that dog so I won't make a mistake and kill him." The man got up from his pallet and said, "Officer, that won't be necessary. It was I who left the scene asking for help from this nice family.

I am going to ask you nicely to please release the man and his son right now," After receiving answers from the man, the officer hands to release Grandpa and Johnny after the man defends them. The man shook Grandpa and Johnny's hands and gave Madea a package before leaving with the sheriff. "Thank you, and I won't forget the promise I made to inform the authorities about problems that may disrupt families on this plantation."

The sheriff opens the car while Grandpa helps the man as he seats him. The sheriff speeds off the plantation just as he comes in. Johnny thought the man might not carry out his word when asking Grandpa and Madea what they thought about the man's integrity. "Gal, do you and Papa think the man will be honest and keep his word as he said he would about the strange happenings around the plantation?"

Madea reassures Johnny and feels the man's sincerity while she converses with him. "I believe the sheriff has already gotten the news from the man, but I am not so sure the sheriff would take it upon himself to take care of this type of trouble," Madea remembers the dream Johnny had when he was much younger, but she declares that it is also her dream that her children will be safe. "I will never let anyone hurt my children, even if I had to die defending them."

Chapter # 11

Unity

Madea insisted that Grandpa would escort the children to and from school until all the pertinent information concerning the unsavory interludes with young males was cleared with the authorities. Grandpa made his business to keep his eyes and ears open to all suspicious entities pertaining to any young child, whether male or female. After weeks of school, Grandpa and Madea thought Johnny and the girls might be out of the way of potential child predators.

With the guidance and teaching that Grandpa and Madea provide for their children and the maturity that Johnny and the girls exemplify, they could be well able to attend school if they heed their parents' instructions and be mindful of new associates and friends. "I think a...ra the danger is within yourself if you forget what Gal and I tell you about the importance of being obedient and how it will haunt you a...ra if you lose sight of it."

Madea agrees with Grandpa and encourages the children to honor what she and Grandpa teach them. " Remember, a hardheaded child brings despair to his life; therefore, it will be wise to keep in mind that there is no one who have your best interest other than Papa and myself." Madea knew the deprivation that the children endured for their ages, although there was a need to explore and welcome other challenges that may cross their paths.

She knew keeping them focused on what was essential during a depression was challenging for her and Grandpa. "Honey, we have so many obstacles at this time. I have a strange instinct about how we are dealing with the lives of these children. "Grandpa had a puzzling and bewildered thought. Madea spoke with irony; his idea of giving the older children curfews might be life-sustaining rather than having heartfelt emotions.

"Gal, you know how I a...ra fill about the protection of Johnny and the girls, and if we give them too much freedom, there might be danger awaiting them." Madea thought speaking to Grandpa privately was a time to reflect on what their options as parents were. She also has reservations about sheltering the children, especially Johnny. Madea gave Grandpa the utmost respect for his opinions and ideas because he demonstrates firmness and is very tactful when dealing with obedience.

"Honey, I love how you handle the little ones, and their manner is a result of experienced rearing that come from generations of love and submissiveness. On the other hand, as they have grown, it is wise that our tactics change according to their maturity. I am not complaining about the way you demand respect, obedience, and character among all of your children, but I believe there is a time to let go in a way of allowing them to observe life's challenges."

Immediately, Grandpa saw how much the subject of allowing Johnny and his sisters to express themselves meant to Madea. She reflects on such an issue of sincere pride and intimacy regarding each of the older children individually. She desires to talk about the future of the older siblings as it behooves her and Grandpa to discontinue sheltering those who are so mature.

"Gal, a...ra you know how I want the children to grow and become productive citizens, but we have an ongoing problem amidst us during this rationing period. There is distrust among some of our neighbors, the sheriff, and the Steindlers." Madea' idea of letting go and giving the children space was a way of teaching them how to enjoy life in a way that did not hinder their growth.

"I can see how the older children have their interest over the years, including Johnny, and how he wants to associate himself with other people, but the sheltering may become something that will imprison them. They will secretly accomplish those things that they desire without our permission. With all the respect and obedience, the children displays, I believe that there are times each of them want their unique space.

I am afraid the older children may act independently to accomplish what they want without our support or permission. Knowing what is going on in our midst will help us understand what we are up against. Therefore, we must teach the children to use their own wit and tolerance, and they will be fine. Those attributes that we instill in them as two parents are very special.

They know an enemy is out there and desires to hurt them. They will use their conscience, the one that will tell them the right from wrong that all of us secretly possess. There will come a time when neither you nor myself will be around to heal their hurt and setbacks. I will never lead the children to a fire if in my heart I know that they are not prepared to quench it and go on living."

Grandpa has always taken Madea's wisdom into account, but he is fighting with mixed emotions. He is not sure whether his acceptance will keep his family safe. Johnny and his sisters continue their walk to school miles away from the plantation every day while Madea and Grandpa work.

They work to provide those needful items for the family, such as essential things, because medical, dental, and childcare are a rarity. The family made a tough decision as they uncovered the news that they may discontinue the children's education until the depression seizes. "Papa, I know it will hurt the children because telling them of our decisions about finalizing their schooling is hurting me.

I promise with all I have within in me that they will succeed in this life. "Grandpa calls all the children to the dinner table about the special announcement. He gave the children the news about the final week of school. "I know a...ra you children have taken to learning a lot of book sense, but you're Momma, and I got to call you home for a while. You a...ra will finish this term, and as a family, we all will take to the field because the babies need someone to mind them."

Johnny was very perturbed from the news because he and the girls came to acquaint themselves with others while getting an education. "Papa, what about my friends and how long this will last, and why can't I just go by myself?" Grandpa thought it was a risk to send any of the children out and walking miles without the security of each other. "I will hear of a...ra no more. I have made my decision; therefore, you will do as I say."

The children continued their timely venture back and forth to school. Grandpa thought as siblings, the children would not stray away from the protection of each other during their walk from the long journey. "I a...ra want each of you to be the others eyes and ears and remember to come home as you left, do not listen to strangers, only that of the one who is rendering you book learning."

Madea thought Grandpa forbade the children to reach out as he prohibited them from associating with others. She knew this might be the beginning of a disastrous relationship for Johnny because of his previous indication of self-will. Grandpa exhibits extreme structure, especially for Johnny; in doing so, Johnny's determination meant going against grandpa and taking a risk to unleash him from continued sheltering.

"Honey, do you think putting such a hold on the children is wise? I believe we may be pushing Johnny too hard, and he might not understand the difference between obedience and obtaining freedom. Please consider this and know that I also urge the children to obey, but I feel that a child may feel trapped if not given a chance to explore their own visions. I am just as responsible for this family as you are, and I would never rule against your sayings in their presence.

We know that there might be a chance that Johnny or the girls will find themselves in a tight position if they travel alone, but we can offer some kind of assurance that the children when approached, will remember those attributes that come with our love for them from childhood rearing. In as much as I can say, they are well-behaved and do not need to be held back in fear or lack.

On the other hand, in order to reach out to peers and acquaintances, Johnny may engage himself in troubling situations without knowing how he comes upon them. I pray that throughout the sheltering these children has endured, they might be strong and know the difference between right and wrong no matter what might come their way." Grandpa began to listen intensely to Madea's plea to lighten up on the children; but he thought the children might waste away without strict discipline and become nothing.

"Gal a...ra we have to allow only the things that are necessary right now because of the rationing period, we have to let the children see that a...ra their time and space, as well as their willingness to adhere to what is going on around them in regards to undue trouble concerning young boys, is important.

When I found Johnny all beaten up and left all tattered and scorn by the white boy and his father, I wanted to kill somebody; not to mention when that bastard hit my son with that damn bat as I watched; I knew that it had to be some level of protection in this family.

I a...ra, will never allow this kind of hurt to reign in our lives. Please a...ra, Gal let me give Johnny and the girls the protection to help them stay alive." Madea knew that Grandpa's idea of family protection would not help the older children. She saw the desires in their body language, and she knew that it was time to let go and simply allow the children to take what she and Grandpa, as parents, had taught from childhood and break away from the cocoon that was bounding them.

The children will in no way ever bind themselves to the strictness that Grandpa has set for them. She has already seen this in Johnny when he develops his own time to play and get to know other people his age at the work site during the field chore. Madea had premonitions of what may happen to Johnny and the rest of the family if their discipline is always among the walls and not by a simple conversation.

She decided to leave the conversation that she and Grandpa had with unity among the two of them and let their relationship continue to be filled with mixed emotions no matter how much it hurt her way down inside. She knew this might destroy a healthy family when two adults cannot come to a compromising situation.

I often knew what Madea meant when she said "try hard to be submissive to your husband no matter how hard the emotion might get;" this is a principle from the bible. I also can relate to her when she says, "In time, we will unify ourselves accordingly." She found the time to nurture Johnny and his sisters without overshadowing them, but seemingly, at an interval, it appears to Grandpa that his firmness solidifies him as the head of the house.

There are times Johnny would take his pet Bob to the field and play games while he trains him; this was an escape for Johnny in an effort to release him from the house. Johnny often hears other children as they scream and play in the field. Johnny hears his name call from one of the children, a nickname that was given him while he worked the field, "Papa Joe," the voice repeats several times, "Papa Joe, come and play."

Without hesitation, Johnny and his dog Bob make their way through the path disregarding Grandpa's plea to obey. Grandpa had no reason to chastise his children at this time, but he only gave them fair warning because of what they may experience. Johnny had no clue that Grandpa was nearby and that he knew everything, even the enticement of the children in the field.

It was very cool from the March morning frost and air, but Johnny resisted the temperature and went toward the beckoning just for a glimpse of the excitement. "Papa Joe, come on and bring your dog right now." Johnny remembers something very special Madea says about asking for permission no matter how hard the temptation is and how this may prove his credibility as a person one day in obtaining future acceptance.

"I cannot go too far away from my house because my papa needs to know where I am at all times, and I need to ask him first, and maybe I can come to play just for a little while." The children continue to make advances at Johnny to do the wrong thing when he has strict words to mind his parents. "I will be back after breakfast; just wait and see." Johnny turns around to the direction of the path as he made his way back into the shack.

"Gal can we eat now? I will make sure the heifer is milked and fed." Madea knew without Johnny even murmuring a word of permission to meet with his friends. "Well, young man I believe I can tell what the excitement is about, so let's wait until Papa comes inside to have his coffee and biscuits." Grandpa came in shortly after Johnny with an arm full of wood for the wood-burning stove.

"Papa, can I help you with the wood? Can I get more to bring in for the fireplace?" Madea hopes Grandpa would reconsider his strictness and allow Johnny to enjoy his childhood with his new friends as Johnny unselfishly remembers the warning given by Grandpa. After the family suppressed their appetites, Johnny started a conversation about playing outside of the yard beyond the field where the children his age were people playing games, wrestling and simply having fun.

"Papa, if I have Bob for protection, may I please go just once and play some fun games with my friends today after chores are done?" Grandpa was very stern about his decision because of past and unsightly situations interrupting his family's space on the plantation. A...ra son, I am very proud of you because you stood up to those guys and said I need to ask for a...ra permission." You may wrestle with your friends only on the inside of the plantation and a...ra none farther, with Bob at your side."

Grandpa was a man of his word. When he spoke, he emphasized his tone. Although he stuttered, his voice was demanding, and each sibling remembers what he says from the toddlers to the family's oldest member. "Please a...ra don't let me come and get you because of the night a...ra falling on you." Johnny tries so hard to win Grandpa's approval.

"Thank you, Papa. I will come home and help with the late chores." After leaving for the park, Johnny ran as if this may be the last time he would be granted time to function away from the shack. He took Bob as a protector and a reminder of what Grandpa instilled in him. Madea knew that Grandpa would do anything for her, even to give the children allegiance a duty to prove themselves of a given task.

She knew that this was a chance for Johnny to grow as an individual, and the very thing they had mixed emotions about would become wholesome and unselfish.

Chapter # 12

"Laughter, Just Waiting To Burst"

Grandpa made it plain that he expected all chores to be done first, with no fun and games until everything was in place. When Bob saw Johnny running about the space, making the rounds, milking the heifer, feeding the chickens, loading the wood, and simply taking in accounts of important chores, he barked as if desiring to help in his own way. Okay, obviously, Bob is a dog, and dogs cannot help with chores, or so it seems; Bob felt the need to be loyal.

He has no prior training in this affair but needs Johnny's attention. Bob knew exactly where the family kept the pails for receiving the heifer's milk. He grabbed the handle of the pail, ran to the shed, and began to bark convincingly to demand to work the heifer. Bob is a gentle pet; there are no intimidations among any of the animals around the space. The cat or even the chickens are friends to Bob and tolerate his fussing.

Grandpa heard a loud rumbling sound coming from the shed as though pots and pans had fallen to the ground. He alerts Johnny, and they run to the shed to what was amidst them in pairs. "Good God a...ra Almighty, get out of here you son of a gun." He chuckles with extreme amazement as he finds Bob covered in manure and dust from the feeding trough. Johnny burst with laughter, but he was disappointed with Bob for creating such a mess. "Ha, ha, I bet you won't look for trouble anymore. Now I've got to clean you up and this mess, too."

Madea and the girls come to see Bob's performance with the heifer. The girls laughed so hard that they all fell excitedly to their knees. It was so hilarious to see such a mess Johnny had to clean up. Madea was so overwhelmed with laughter that she and

Grandpa knew exactly what motivated Bob behind the mess. "Listen, children, I believe Bob has met his match, but he simply wants to help.

The heifer did not need an amateur to engage in milking her. Bob wants the attention of all of us, especially Johnny; He does things to please Johnny because of his loyalty. He will always show his love and friendship to Johnny as long as he lives. Yes, Johnny, you have a big mess here, but you will not be cleaning it alone. The girls and I will show our love for Bob and help clean up everything while Johnny cleans Bob."

Johnny knew his hands would be filled for the next few days, training Bob in behavior etiquettes. He did not expect Grandpa to overlook what happened in regards to Bob aggravating the herd and causing a huge mess for the family to clean up. "Come here, Bob. We may start now because this will be one of my next chores in keeping you away from the yard animals."

Grandpa had a different perspective of Bob and what took place around the heifer; he was delighted to know he had a new helper. It was quite contrary to what Johnny had in mind about training Bob to behave. Grandpa thought it was hilarious to see the loyalty in one pet dog. Grandpa saw the hurt in Bob's behavior when he did not receive a pleasing reception from Johnny. "

Johnny a...ra what are you doing? No matter what you do, you could never a...ra change a pet when all he wants to do is please his master. There will come a time when that very bobtail animal will help you out of a very sticky situation. So let us give Bob what he was looking for and show him how to help instead of routing him out." Johnny thought Grandpa's actions were very unusual from what he assumed because of his intolerance of him and his siblings.

He appreciates Grandpa's lectures and dedicates what he learns today to his pet, Bob. Good boy Bob let's fetch the pail, and I will help you; we will do this together. Grandpa left Johnny with Bob and went back to his business as he prepared for work. "Okay, do not mess with the heifer; just bring me the pails." Johnny had so much fun with Bob as he tended his chores with his pet at his side.

He teased him and created silly and awkward things just for a laugh. Johnny took the time to train Bob as they got closer. This was a convenience whereas; he found just what he needed inside his immediate surroundings. "We are not done yet. Let's gather some firewood, one piece at a time."

Madea was amazed to see Johnny so happy and full of life, but she knew even this would only last for a "season," meaning time spent with Bob is good while he is young and strong, but a pet's life span ends as the wind blows and the leaves fall. Madea takes all things into consideration when rearing the children. She and the girls made pork sandwiches and sweet lemon water for Johnny to celebrate the happy moment that Bob created for the family with a burst of laughter.

"Come on, girls, let's go outside and make Johnny feel that he is not alone and that he can rely on us as a family. We will contribute to the chores." Madea knew Johnny was shy about jugging the heifer, but she allowed him to feel a sense of responsibility just for growth. "Johnny, you know how much we appreciate your help around the yard, so if there is something we may help with, please let us know."

Johnny was so happy to see Madea and the girls out in the open space for a change; he welcomed the help and made provisions for the toddler to play in plain view. "Oh, Gal, if we may start with the heifer, I will ensure the buckets are clean and ready to receive her milk." The second oldest girl, the dramatic one, decides to play a joke on Johnny. As she sat on the can to milk the heifer, she called out to Johnny, "Hey, little brother, may I give you some pointers in milking a heifer?"

Johnny was simply astonished because this meant the more he knew about jugging the heifer would be a lot quicker for him to complete his task. I see; lately, we haven't had any milk. Do you really know how it's done?" Johnny always felt he had to prove his male image to the girls. "Well, sort of." Madea knew exactly what was about to happen. She spoke up on Johnny's behalf and said, "Let everybody take a chance at jugging the heifer."

She asked the girls to start so Johnny could see his mistakes and can learn from them. "The outspoken, dramatic one asked Johnny to see the milk come as she worked the heifer. Johnny got on his knees in such amazement to enjoy the very act, and in his face splatters the milk from the heifer. Madea filled with laughter. She could hardly sustain herself. After all the excitement, Madea reminds Johnny never sat under a heifer or stand behind her during the milking process because it can be unsafe for him as it was for Bob, his pet dog.

The girls were all inquisitive about how Johnny comes to complete all chores if the heifer intimidates him. "Yes, little brother, and how did you fool us into thinking you did all the chores, including jugging the heifer?" Grandpa made sure Johnny and his siblings learned to focus while they learned. "Your papa is a very wise and patient man; he will never put anything on you that you cannot handle.

I knew that after he continued jugging the heifer and asking Johnny to carry the milk inside, he would know when it was time to leave him to work the heifer all by himself as he did the fieldwork. I am very proud of Johnny for doing the best he can with chores, and one day he will become an expert in juggling the heifer as we are. Remember, son animals are very sensitive and need gentle treatment.

Now, I have a thing or two to say to you girls, and please let us make no mistake that what I say is not that I am partial or impartial to any of my children. This is only a learning experience for all who may be concerned. We are not to make joking remarks to each other, especially if the opposite party is trying to educate himself in any area of life. Come now, I got a pot of stew on the stove because Papa will be coming home for a bite for lunch, and we have a lot to tell him about our fun with the heifer."

Madea knew Johnny had a lot of maturing to do, but she always said "in time, all will be gathered," This meant that Johnny had a lifetime to learn to jug the heifer."

Chapter # 13

Gone Fishing

Johnny was quite puerile when it comes to women's privacy; he regards milking a cow as tampering with female breast, which seems disgusting to him. This may seem trivial or silly to other members of the family, but Johnny thought this chore was for grownups. He was not quite there yet. He made a vow to himself that he would show the family that he could jug the heifer with no problem, but every time he came near her, she would swing her tail and move as if abused by an assailant.

Johnny knew this was a chore for everyone, including the youngest sibling, as their maturity allowed them. He began to reminisce about previous conversations he and Madea had about the treatment of animals by repeating to himself, saying, "I know I could do this because Gal says to be gentle, and that is what I will be." Johnny sat on the upside-down pail, closed his eyes, and started to count. "One, two, and three, I will do this; they will see."

Johnny took both hands with his eyes still shut tight and began to pull and Jug the heifer, and milk came with consistent streams. He continues with the process and nervously says in a very calm voice, "Thank you, girl." After filling both pails, he knew there was nothing he could not accomplish."I knew I could, and I did so, all by myself just like Gal says to do."

After completing the chore, Johnny starts toward the shack with extreme relief as though the Rock of Gibraltar was lifted off his back. He carries both filled pails up the steps and into the doorway with pride. Grandpa and Madea knew Johnny would milk the heifer; they allowed him to prove to himself and build his confidence in himself. Shortly after Johnny enters the shack,

Grandpa comes in behind him with a line of fish waiting to be scaled and cleaned.

This chore was strictly for the girls, but Johnny insisted on cleaning fish and simply assuming all chores to prove his manhood. "Papa, look; I have accomplished a lot today! She let me jug her; the heifer really let me jug her. Now, I am going to continue the rest of the chores with this string of fish all by myself." Grandpa calls for the girls to assist with his catch by attending their special chores.

"Son, it is a...ra wise to remember that all a...ra chores are taken up with me and Gal. Come in a...ra now, and wash up for supper. The females are fast a...ra with their fingers and will have supper on the table before you can a...ra count to three." The cows' milk and fish were perishable items and only had a limited time before discarding. Whatever the family did not consume at one meal, the rest chills with block ice securing the family's food source.

Five cents during the Depression was a challenge for most families to come across, even to purchase ice to keep their food from going bad. Madea takes the initiative to save without a warrant. She manages to find a corner to store a penny or two in a private collection after she gives it to her church.

"When I pay a tenth of what I am blessed, I will rest assured that (He) will come in my defense every time."She knew that something about giving had always given her a sense of pleasure, even if it was all she had. "Hurry, girls, your Papa must be starving after catching this big bounty of a blessing. Johnny, you may pour the milk into the ice chest so there will be milk for the babies in the morning."

Madea slices the cooking lard for the fish as the girls wash and season the catch. She prepares the bread on top of the wood-burning stove just as Grandpa likes it all in a hoecake. The family sat and gave thanks for their meal and began to enjoy their feast. Madea candidly speaks but not hesitant nor selfishly and says,

"Papa, now this is way too much for us to eat alone; we must take a basket and share our goods among somebody."

We will not waste anything, but we are going to offer a little kindness to our neighbor because one day, that same spirit of love may find its way back into our lives. The second oldest the dramatic one, reminds Madea of a previous gift when she says, "Gal, do you remember the huge basket that the Mrs gave us filled with presents?" Madea, filled with excitement and purpose, said, "Oh yes, it is a beautiful piece of handiwork."

Grandpa knew how much the children, even Madea, loved the beautiful artistry from the Stiendlers and began to intervene; "this is a gift a...ra from the Stiendlers to you; now let's a...ra offer our neighbor a gift from us. I have just the thing, and it is just as nice, so let me a...ra run out to the shed and get it." Bob growls and barks as, alerting the family of a visitor. Johnny was quite anxious because he did not want to lose another pet.

"Oh, Papa, somebody is here because Bob is ready to fight." When Grandpa stood up, there was a knock at the door. He made his way to the door, and surprisingly, Mr. Steindler's son with the same artistry of baskets that the Mrs gave to the family as a precious gift. "I came to deliver these items to you from my father, who has passed.

We found them in these special baskets with this letter from Mother. I hope you are making it well considering the depression, and I hope this was not too big of a burden for you, and I will be in touch again." Grandpa receives the gifts, invites the young Mr. Steindler to the shack, and offers some of his catch. "Oh, thanks, but I must not impose on your supper." Grandpa insists that Mr. Steindler must eat with his family. "We a...ra have more than we could possibly consume. The catch-a-ra...ra was a huge blessing today."

Mr. Steindler laughs and says, "I believe I came at the right time. I am famished, but I have other members of the family that awaits me in the car." Madea removes herself from the table and politely brings a basket filled with hoecakes and fish for the Steindler's; Mr. Steindler please take this basket so you may have a picnic, and I hope you enjoy what we enjoy. Our love and prayers extend to you and your family for the loss of your father. He will be greatly missed."

Mr. Steindler thanks Madea and Grandpa once more. "It's a pleasure. I hope we all get through what's seemingly the worst depression of all times; I do thank you for your goods." The children were ecstatic because it seemed just as Madea said, but they did not think it would happen so quickly. That spirit of love came just minutes for the family.

Madea accepts the gifts, but she exhibits genuine sympathy for the Steindlers. "I did not know that the Mr. was so sick. I have not heard from the family since we were informed about the changes in our stay at the shack. I wish I could give back a portion of what the Mr. and Mrs. have given to me even in their departure. I will always remember and cherish our friendship." Madea began to sob uncontrollably when she placed the gifts on the table.

Grandpa held Madea's hands and said, "Come a...ra Gal, I don't think the Mr. and Mrs. will have you a...ra grieving like this." Madea accepts Grandpa's efforts to console her and says, "It must be a reason why we enjoyed such a huge supply of fish, and I believe it came today. We shared the food and enjoyed a brief moment with Mr. Steindler. I believe this may be the start of a good relation between families. The Mr. and Mrs. are exhibiting their love for us even in their eternal sleep."

Chapter # 14

"Patience"

"Come, children, there is something for each of us. We will share in the moment of giving and receiving." Madea made sure the family understood why there was a sudden arrival of love knocking at the door. "When I was a girl, my parents looked for ways to give, even when they did not have anything at all. My mother cooked and washed for her neighbor, and Papa helped pull crops just because they had a desire to give.

The Steindler's are gone, but look what a blessing we have because of their love. They made sure their son finds the gifts and delivered them to us; these are two gifts: friendship and sharing." Johnny plans to show off his new hunting boots as his patience was wearing thin just to greet his friends.

The girls, including Madea, each had cloaks with embroidered tapestry; the toddlers wore head bonnets, and Grandpa never thought putting on a pair of new denim overalls was possible. These gifts made him feel like a real man who can give his family just a sample of life's pleasure. The oldest sibling seems curious of how the sizes were exact. "Gal, did you tell the Mrs. 's son that we needed these valuables, and how did he know our favorite colors?"

Madea reminds the children that these things were a part of the Mrs. Vision each time she drops off the dirty laundry and receives them weekly. "Do you remember when you met the Mrs., and she ask lots of questions and gave you gifts of books and toys? These are wonderful gifts that we might not otherwise accumulate ourselves. She knew there would come a time when we could use these gifts.

Your Papa and I are in a compromising situation; we had plans to cancel school for the term until the depression ends. I do not know if it is wise to continue as planned or send you back right now. All I know is that you are far behind in your studies; I will talk to Papa tonight, and we will solve this problem."The two oldest girls and Johnny, too, answer politely and nonresistant in unison, "Yes, mam."

Madea made sure things were in place and tidy. "Let us get out of our best things and get ready for another day we will have plenty of time to show off our gifts." Madea knew that Mrs encourages schooling no matter how much an economic blitz may be upon the family. She would say, "Now, Bell, you can't shut the children out from the world; they need lots of book sense; you've got to make sure that has to be done."

After the family retires for bed, Madea and Grandpa climb into bed before blowing out the lamp. "Well, I thought you may hear what the children and I discussed last evening." Grandpa interrupts Madea slightly and said, "I know, and I a...ra want the same thing." In a surprising tone, Madea had high hopes for this answer.

Grandpa knew Madea's dream for the children's education, and there could be no better time to take a leap of faith. I will a...ra honor your decision in what is best for a...ra Johnny and the girls returning to school anytime." Madea laughs and says, "You ole rascal, you knew all the time that this was on my mind."

When Madea and Grandpa received the news about Mr. Steindlers' father, he saw the devastation in Madea's eyes and knew that there was nothing she would do to please the Mrs. at that very moment. "I a...ra knew from a...ra the start that it pleases you knowing the children can continue with their studies with both of our approvals."

Madea and Grandpa continued talking about their decision until they each fell asleep. The next day, the children rush out of bed along with Madea and ask, "Well, Gal, what did Papa say, and when will we start." Madea wants the children to realize that no matter what the outcome of their conversation, they must exhibit patience.

"When Papa comes to the morning meal, we will lay down our special rules about what we expect from each of you and how important it is that you are careful, knowing that there is still trouble amongst us. At this time, we want the utmost respect and obedience from all our children."

Johnny thought this was the time for him to mingle with boys his age and accomplish what Madea and Grandpa had set for him and his sisters. He was excited about going back to his studies and seeking new friends. "Okay, children, we have chores to do. Johnny, hurry and fetch the wood for breakfast, and girls, you know your chores. Let's get some eggs and milk." Grandpa finally awoke yawning like a roaring lion waiting for pampering and pleasing by his precious girls. "Papa, here is your coffee mug, and may I get your slippers." Madea and Grandpa decide to give the children their answers together at breakfast. "I a...ra want more out of life for my a...ra children, that is why I am sending each of you back to get more book learning.

Remember chores done a...ra after you reach home. Do a...ra my children, not tarry." Grandpa was very stern about what he said, but Madea often warns the siblings about trusting her and Grandpa and doing the right thing. "Children, we are still in a serious depression. Work is bare, and there is not enough food even to feed the animals, so please be mindful of what we expect each of you to do."

Madea started by asking each child about their responsibility after the long walks from school; she thought of using a little elementary psychology. "So, Johnny, what are your chores upon reaching the plantation?" Johnny knew the consequences of not fulfilling his chores, so he took great pleasure in giving Madea his list of duties. "Gal, after I am done with chores, I will join you and Papa in the field."

Madea did not have such an unction about the girls as she had with Johnny; it is not that Madea favored or trusted the girls more, but she knew there was a common enemy out there, the one that tries to ponder the mind of even the most mannered and tolerable child a family may have. The girls gave their list of responsibilities and said, "We will find you in the field and gather the baby and the toddlers after all chores are done."

Madea simply wanted the children to arrive unharmed after school. "After breakfast, we will help Papa gather the slop for the animals. I believe we will have a great year despite the depression causing our food shortage." Grandpa had great optimism about what he thought the outcome would possess. There may be a...ra a food shortage, but my family will never a... ra miss a meal. We will have enough to give our neighbor. Yes, a...ra, I have seen worst, but we somehow a...ra made it."

Chapter # 15

A Pivotal Moment

Madea kept thinking about her and Grandpa's conversation with the drifter, informing them of an apparent situation involving juveniles. She always knew that there is a reason why things become knowledge. She and Grandpa relied on the drifter's word when he said he would inform the authorities of what he experienced. Now, it has settled in their minds that the sheriff knows about the agonizing drama and has declared justice for such malice.

Johnny was only twelve at that time, and who would think a crime could persist for such a lengthy period? Madea and Grandpa have erased all the significance of this estranged and impromptu plot of evil in the lives of their family, or they simply become complacent in pursuing things that can haunt them for the rest of their natural lives. "I can see how the children are doing well and happy about their surroundings.

"Do you remember when the drifter came relying on our assistance for his untimely mishap and informed us of the evil that may invade the lives of our children?" Grandpa has always thought of defending the rights of his family; he who lives by the sword ultimately will die accordingly. Grandpa spoke with undesirable languages but not a grammar issue; he slightly stutters as usual.

"I will a...ra die first before I a...ra let some mother fucker a...ra hurt my children. I will fight until I win." Madea was afraid of his answers and knew she should remain calm with all her strength no matter what infringement she had to endure. She spoke quite candidly and said, "Oh honey, I never for once saw you as a husband and father who would let your family down.

Please let us forget about weapons and bad words for now and be thankful." Madea knew she would have to make restitution for any trouble that may come their way. She loves Grandpa and has long needed him to be the husband, father, and confidant. "I think the children will be fine; they a...ra have traveled those paths for over two years, and we had no problems.

I think the sheriff a...ra done put an end to this ordeal; besides, Johnny knows what to do if trouble comes." With all the rearing and love, children sometimes tend to have their own will and, therefore, would explore with no intent of disrupting normal protocol. Madea knew Johnny is a hot head when it came to his family, just like his father, and this was not safe, especially at a tender age like his.

She whispers to herself as she mumbles without speaking directly to an audience, "I need more of an assurance that all is well." Grandpa and Madea knew the only way to move forward was to focus on what was ahead, knowing that there may be trouble, but with love for each other, they will persevere to the end. Johnny and the girls took to school as often as there were school days.

Each time the children come and go, they contribute to their chores as planned. Madea saw a slight difference in Johnny's demeanor; he made certain remarks concerning his new associates. She knew Johnny would fight from certain experiences and that he takes no intimidation. "Please, my son, if you need to inform your Papa and me of something, we urge you not to hesitate."

Johnny thought he could continue his routine venture with friends after school, but things took a twist in the twinkle of an eye. His life would change drastically. After the school doors shut, the children could return home or to their appropriate destinations until the next day.

Johnny ran out ahead of his sisters, making every moment count; he had no idea that he was setting himself up for a common trap, a disaster with others, he did not realize that this would be the last time he may see his family. The girls waited patiently for their only brother; they knew returning to the plantation without one sibling would cause strife among the family.

"Oh, where is he? Where is Johnny!" The girls made every effort to search for Johnny but had no luck. "He must be found before we get to the shack. What will we tell Gal and Papa!" After returning home, the girls went straight to the field where Grandpa, Madea, and the younger siblings were as they normally did, but this time they had a bit of disturbing news to give their parents.

The oldest spoke first; Papa, Gal, Johnny ran out ahead, and we could not find him anywhere; we stayed and looked for him. Grandpa spoke quite stern and said, "Knowing a...ra Johnny, he will be moseying a...ra on home soon. We will give him time." Madea simply knew something was not quite right, "How long have you been looking for your brother? Have you gone to the shack?" The girls looked ghastly, "No, Gal, we were scared. We came straight here after leaving the schoolyard.

We found Johnny's lunch pail all bent up and stumped on. Madea began to hum the kind of hum they do in church when that sad song gets hold of them. "Gal, just take it easy a...ra we will be getting back to the shack now." Madea had gathered peas with a lap filled all day as she placed them in her apron to store each bundle before emptying them in the holding sacks.

She rose from her knees, stood, and said, "Please protect my child." Forgetting all the work she sacrificed, Madea simply loses focus, and all the peas fall to the ground. Grandpa rushed to her side when she began to lose her ability to stand straight, as she seemed to be fainting.

Grandpa yells out at the girls, "Ya'll gather the babies and a...ra come on!"Grandpa takes hold of Madea as she props her head on his shoulder and gently walks through the paths and out of the field while the two older siblings gather the toddlers and the younger child. "Gal, do you remember a...ra what I said about you and a...ra the children and how I will fight to protect you?

Madea simply shook her head and said softly, "I hope Johnny's home, my son; please be home." The space had a calm and serene solitude; everything was in place, the way Grandpa and Madea left things, even Bob lying patiently in his kennel.

When Grandpa realized what he was up against, all things began to unravel, and there was so much tension, chores to be done, hungry children, and Grandpa wanted to get his old antique rifle as chaos brews the entire night. "Honey, please put that away; we don't know whether the sheriff will come and tell us about Johnny; all I know is that he is out somewhere and needs our help.

I feel like a part of me is gone. I feel so sick inside, but I know that we need to be strong right now." After Grandpa and the girls secured the chores, Madea set the table as if Johnny were about to enter the meal. "I a...ra will borrow the mule and buggy tomorrow."

Madea knew Grandpa's idea of protecting his family was vengeance; she believed that at any given time, Grandpa's hurt and pain will surface, and ultimately, he would unload his anger. "We should all get some sleep now because there may be a great deal of pressure coming our way; we will be alert and on our best behavior, will gather food and water for our trip. I believe tomorrow is going to be a long and exhausting day for all of us."

When Grandpa opened his eyes the next day, Madea had breakfast ready for the toddlers, the baby and the whole family. She sacrificed herself to remain calm no matter how bad her pain persists without Johnny around. "Gal, a...ra will you stay home and rest? I will take our neighbors with me for a...ra support."

The girls agree with Grandpa, but Madea does not hear of it. "I dream of holding my son, my only son, next to my breath, so I must be there when we set out; we should all be there for Johnny." Grandpa did not exchange words. He left without a moment's notice and fetched the neighbor's mule and buggy. "Gal, do you think Johnny is at fault by disobeying you and Papa, and should he suffer the consequences that he imposes on himself?

I remember the very words you and Papa often preaches about disobeying the elders." Madea was very adamant about what she said to her family. She made sure the girls understood her. "This might not be Johnny's fault; I know my son, and he would never intentionally disobey your Papa or me. Wherever Johnny is at this very moment, he is hurting just like we are."

The dramatic sibling spoke with sincere urgency after gently kissing Madea. "Gal, I have a poem to recite. It is not a sad one; it's just a time of reassurance, and it goes like this: We are all together in a quiet and no vengeful endeavor. Besides, I spoke to Johnny, and he is over-talking somebody; isn't that funny? He knows the anguish surrounding his absence but stays focused, knowing he has a family of great prominence.

We will always stick out for each other; therefore, all minds will be clear, as the heart will soon catch up and dismiss fear. Little brother, I know you think you know everything, but it is okay. Just be quiet and listen out for Gal as she softly sings.

She will get there just in time to rub your naps, and with your hands, there will be sounds as you clap to observe Gal saying thank you, lord, once more, for you are all full of grace, even for those of us who occupy this sinful shore."

Madea thought at that very moment that she could accomplish anything as she had the propensity to take on any challenge, even as her heart aches for her only son. Madea starts to cry with a sense of relief while she does the humming song. It is not often the toddlers would question Gal or Papa, but there was a little voice just down around Madea's knees, being quite inquisitive, "Gal, why do you cry? Is it because Johnny is gone?

He will be right back soon, just like my raggedy doll you made for. Papa found her when I was sad!" Madea explains to the little tot the reason mothers often cry for their missing children. She began by saying, "When the little chick misses a little bitty, she is often fussy until her bitty is back in her presence.

Johnny was only two years old when I spank him for straying away from my sight. I was scared and could not rest until I found him. This is the love I have, for he is one of my bitties that I will hold dear to my heart. Grandpa finally trots up with the mule and buggy. Madea ran out to the buggy before he prepared the harness for the toddlers and said,

"Honey, I want to see if Johnny might show up on his own, maybe the day after tomorrow, we can make our search. I believe he is trying to make his way home. After days of looking and searching, the schoolyard Madea knew she and Papa should search elsewhere.

Even being the head of the house, Grandpa often relies on Madea's wisdom and prepares to fulfill every suggestion she may have. He harnesses both toddlers while the older sibling sits in the backcourt, minding the baby. Grandpa opens the kennel door, and Bob makes full speed up and into the buggy where he would have occupied his usual space if Johnny had been present.

Grandpa helps Madea to the carriage while she lifts her maxi-length skirt. Madea knew how Johnny stood his ground no matter his situation; she remembered when he and Grandpa had to fight off the bullies at the field protecting their goods.

"I know Johnny will fight, so maybe the sheriff done brought him in, or maybe they will help us find him. oh lord I hope so."

It was a long ride that day, late March, and quite chilly, just days away from Johnny's fourteenth birthday. Madea knows how the white authorities talk to Negroes, especially men, so she pleads with Grandpa to let her enter the jailhouse without him.

"I know how protective you are about your family, but let me go in alone and just remain in the buggy and mind the girls."

Grandpa saw how much this moment meant to Madea he humbled down and said, "I will be a...ra right here if a...ra you come to needing me." Madea was very emotional at this point but, not because she was shy when approaching the sheriff in charge, but because she had great emotional pain because of the disappearance of Johnny.

When Madea entered the building, some unfriendly attendants were very cold and careless. "Come on in, gal, and who do you come to see?" Madea knew that this was the reception for Negroes, so she applied her old way of speaking. "I'ze come to see if they done brung my child down here. I'ze been look'n all day fur my son John Henry Harris.

The sheriff was vain and futile quite ineffective, and had no sympathy for the pain that Madea exhibits for her son. "There ain't no negra boy here by the name of John Henry Harris." The sheriff did not attempt to offer any assistance to help Madea find Johnny. He simply made down-grading remarks concerning the loss of a missing child.

His countenance was trifling disconcerted; "When you find that bastard, you need to beat the shit out of him. Madea could not say anything to let on that she disapproved of the disrespect shown her in searching for her missing child. The sheriff would place her in contempt and lock her up even if she shed a tear. The sheriff continued with his lethargic attitude by mocking Madea as she turned to make her exit, "If we find your boy dead, I will bring him home."

Madea's heart ached; she was agonized and irate, but she made herself a promise that she will find her son Johnny.

Chapter # 16

My Only Son

After Madea left the sheriff's office, she headed towards the buggy, withdrawn and solemn as a heartbroken child. She knew that she was all alone in finding her son Johnny. As much as Grandpa loves his family, Madea thought he was no better off than the cold-hearted sheriff or the ones responsible for his disappearance.

Madea knew that Grandpa would go to any length to settle a dispute, jeopardizing his life or the life of his neighbors even if it meant dying and leaving the ones so dear behind. She whispers to herself as she says in her formal, unfiltered grammar, "I'ze tied, but I will find my chil." Grandpa looked around and saw Madea slowly approaching the buggy, and without tarrying,, he jumped from the buggy, met her, and helped her to the seat.

"Gal, a…ra now tell me what did they say about my son?" Madea replies very softly, "He has not been arrested; they don't have Johnny at the jailhouse. Please take me home, take me home now!" It was a long ride home from the jailhouse and Madea sat quietly wondering if Johnny was warm or if he had food and water. "We will not a…ra stop. We will find Johnny very soon."

The children were saddened and tearful-eyed as they made uplifting comments to elevate Madea's spirit. "Gal, Johnny is around people he knows; He knows how to defend for himself he will be alright." When Grandpa reaches the plantation, Madea asks to be alone as the family returns to the shack. She nostalgically had visions of Johnny and the good times they shared when he were a little tot.

"Just put me out. I like to sit and feel the wind in my hair momentarily. You will find me here when you drop the mule and buggy off to our neighbor." Madea sat in the park and sang; finally, after hearing others talk, she simply listened with anticipation.

When she thought it was a clue as to where Johnny might be, she began to join the conversation but did not let on that her son was missing, too.

"That is a sad thing to do, break up boys from their families. Do you think they will release the boys? Can their parents come and get them?" One of the talkers said, "Where did you come from? You must promise you did not hear this information. Do you know that you can lose your life? Please tell no one because our families are depending on each other for survival, and we are going through a depression, and we can starve to death."

Madea knew immediately that Johnny might be among the captives, but she had to get more information about such an operation. She knew that this was an unjust infringement of any human rights. "Pardon my manners; it just hurts my heart knowing that there may be cruelty among us. I will not mention any of this to my family, but I do not want them wandering off near this site.

At that particular moment, Madea's fate was at the mercy of the strangers. I can simply urge them to steer clear from it if I only knew where it might be." The talkers continue confidently asking, "Do not tell a soul." Madea replied again, "I would keep silent at all cost." "There is a plantation housing young Negro boys against their will to work very hard without wages and stripped of their dignity and freedom.

If you have a young boy, please keep watch on him; make sure he is in the company of others who can run and scream and yell, alerting the trespassers to stay away." After receiving such gravely information, Madea sat and continued to sing.

She thought this was the exact thing the drifter told her and Grandpa of when he came to needing their assistance more than two years prior to Johnny's disappearance, but refused to give credible details. "Where did you hear of such mischief in these parts?"

Finally, Grandpa heads back to the park with the mule and buggy just as planned. Grandpa got out of the buggy and helped Madea to the seat. Madea knew the plantation where she and her family live very well, but she had no idea of any other than the Stiendlers plantation where she makes her daily rounds.

Madea made up a fictitious plot to get Grandpa to walk back from the neighbors to the shack. "Please, if we can just drop off the buggy, and can we walk home?" This would help my spirit at this very moment." Grandpa did just as Madea requested; the pair walked from the neighbor's home and made their way toward the shack.

Madea began to talk about the conversation she had with the people she met in the park; she was not completely honest. She had to steer Grandpa away from what was actually on her mind.

"I want to work my laundry business. A few women know of a plantation owner near this one who may be in need of some washing; this will keep me busy as I stay near the house in case Johnny shows up." Grandpa knew Madea was hurting because the family was missing Johnny, but he had no idea that Madea was planning to take on an awesome adventure for an escape. "I will a...ra take you tomorrow after breakfast."

After the family eats the last meal, they prepare for bed. Madea makes a plan to tell Grandpa of her desire to keep busy. "There won't be any need to take me where the plantation is; just tell me in your own words. I have walked these sites for a long time with my babies, and I believe we will do just fine on our own while you are in the fields."

It was a very cold moment in Madea's life without her only son. She tries to be strong, but each day was like a tyrant trying to take her soul away. For days, Madea would not eat or sleep; she knew she had to come up with a strategy to free Johnny. After weeks of going her mind about what to do when she comes to this plantation holding Negro boys, she begins to sing and hum; she prays that this is, indeed, where Johnny may be.

"I will go on my own, walk to this place where they are holding my child, and rescue him all on my own." Madea makes known to the older children of her compelling desire to go out to bring in work, and she would like to be alone. She lies once more but was indeed convincing. After preparing a basket of changing clothes, she took to the path and strait way, leaving her family behind in pursuit of finding Johnny.

"I must go now. I shall waste no time." It was a very chilly morning and a long stretch for Madea, but she made her way exactly as she planned. Madea stops and removes her formal clothing in exchange for what was in her basket. When she came to what was seemingly the place where Johnny were, she began to cry and sing that old humming song.

Just before Madea entered the gate, she heard a villainous voice calling out, in a Southern twang, "Stop that negra gal." Madea was extremely afraid; she promised to die trying to rescue her only son. One of the assailants comes trotting in a mighty hurry, where she was carrying a shotgun and a bat.

"Now, who sent you here, gal, and who do you need to see?" It comes as no surprise that Madea appears young, just like a teenage girl. She was a beautiful young woman in great shape. "I'ze be cumin to see my main. I'ze misses him and gots to havs a lil lovin. Madea knew that she had to devise a convincing hoax to save herself and her son.

"Well, who would be your man, and who gave you knowledge about the whereabouts of this plantation?" "He be called Johnny," Madea gains access to the plantation by posing as her son's lover. I'ze know nobody; I just want to lay with him, as we need to comfort each other.

After seeing Johnny for the first time in weeks, she knew she had to continue her quest for her family and neighbors' sake. Madea ran to Johnny in a way that gave him first notice of her plot to free him. The overseer shot once in the air as he checked to ensure no weapons were on Madea.

"Come here, woman, heist your skirt up, and let me see what is under there." She did exactly what the overseer asked; she brought nothing but a desire to free her only son. "Now go and be quick!" She tenderly whispers to Johnny, "Be a good boy and do what I'ze says."

The overseer turns away after viewing Madea's half-naked body, as this was a heart-wrenching relief for Madea; she was afraid and quite intimidated by the assailant's action. Madea remembers as a very young child how girls' innocence was taken or sexually assaulted by older assailants' and left with no one to come in their behalf.

The gunman made no advances toward Madea; instead, he went on with his business.

Johnny knew without any doubt that he must help Madea because this was his only hope for both of them. He began to undo his trousers as to give in to temptation only to assist with the plot for freedom, giving more assurance to the gunman that the moment was real intimacy between two people.

Madea knew exactly what her next move was as she continued to release other pieces of the garment. Johnny began to make whispering conversations with his mother. " Trust me, son, and do only what I say." When it was safe, Madea and Johnny made their way toward the gate like two combat soldiers, as they were careful not to alert the assailant or any innocent casualties.

Madea was very cautious; she knew how devastating it was as a girl as she put her life on the line. "There is a hole just towards the opening of the gate as if an animal has made an attempt to enter these grounds; now watch and squat as you see me." Madea was able to ease herself through the hole under the fence, freeing herself.

She was freezing in the March winds with little clothing as she began to whisper to Johnny in a very soft and low-key voice. "Slowly squat, son, and free yourself." Johnny was shaking like a leaf, afraid that he'd be jammed. "Now do what I say, John Henry Harris, again squat and squat Now!"

Johnny began to remember briefly how he reached confidence in himself simply by listening to his mother as he learned how to milk the heifer. "I can do this." "Yes, you can, my son; we don't have even a second to linger!" Johnny knew he must obey his mother and allow himself to be the one she was depending on at that very moment.

He was a bit larger than his mother and extremely taller, but he was able to get free from the locked fence. "Slowly stand, Johnny; now run, son, and don't look back."

They began to run, and they ran until they were completely out of site. With tears in her eyes, Madea cried out, "Thank You, God, for giving back my only son. I did not speak us come out live.

THE END

ACKNOWLEDGEMENTS

I listened to an experience so inspirational, yet tear-jerking about one so dear to me, my grandmother, Isabella Lee Harris, whom touched me immensely. Isabella is referred to as Gal by her husband and children, and her grandchildren, grandnieces, and nephews are referred to as Madea. Madea left a legacy of love built around caring for her family and taking perilous risks for the sake of them as well. It was at a family gathering when one so passionate, filled with spiritual integrity, and touched by a compelling desire to reminisce about the trials that led her to tell those whom are among the descendants about a disadvantaged period in their lives when there was little or no voice at all. I remembered the very words expressed to me by Madea as she told me about how a mother of nine siblings' Uncle Johnny being the third oldest child, and the tragic death of one two-year-old toddler. The devastation of not containing the ability to have medical facilities available was callous and brutal. Food and school suddenly became a rarity, and so did simple necessities. When caring for the younger children, a filled belly superseded education. Madea worked the fields when sharecropping fed her family while the older sibling kept watch in babysitting the younger children. She was very passionate about the welfare of the children; even though there were few, she would take scraps and prepare sufficient amounts for all. She taught her children to waste nothing but to offer kindness to their neighbors; one day, that spirit of love returns to them. The family lived in a single-dwelling house with a high and elevated crawl space, making access convenient as the drayman dumps useful food beneath the floor. These were perishable items and other needed goods that contributed to the family's food shortage. When school was possible, Uncle Johnny and his sisters walked miles and miles from the plantation to their school, and Uncle Johnny loved to wander off after school to interact with other boys, although being warned to stay with his sisters, as they were safer in numbers. Madea often expressed to her children that "obedience is a key to longevity and hard headiness brings on a soft ass,"; meaning if you willingly disobeyed the elders, there may be serious consequences to pay.

ABOUT THE AUTHOR

Born Janice Perry in Brooks County Quitman Georgia, during infancy her parents moved near relatives and friends to Dougherty County Albany Georgia. Being under her mother's guardianship, she assumed her mothers' present last name as Reynolds despite what has written on her birth certificate and recognized as Janice Reynolds all her childhood life. She later married and became known as Janice Sibley but to some she dropped the name of Sibley and again assumed the name of Janice Reynolds

Janice Reynolds lives in the area of Lee County, Georgia. Janice's co-workers gave her the nickname Jani Mae during her working career because there was no middle name. She likes to attain her name as Jani Perry as written on her birth certificate as author and as a name given and signed by her father at birth.

She is a graduate of Kaplan University in Buena Vista Florida, and a retiree. She started writing her first book after receiving an associate degree in Business Administration during which she took an interest in literary art.

www.ingramcontent.com/pod-product-compliance
Lightning Source LLC
LaVergne TN
LVHW051554080426
835510LV00020B/2972